Visual Basic
Sample Codes

by Dr. Liew Voon Kiong

Disclaimer

Visual Basic Sample Codes is an independent publication and is not affiliated with, nor has it been authorized, sponsored, or otherwise approved by Microsoft Corporation.

Trademarks

Microsoft, Visual Basic, Excel, Access and Windows are either registered trademarks or trademarks of Microsoft Corporation in the United States and/or other countries. All other trademarks belong to their respective owners.

Liability

The purpose of this book is to provide a basic guide for people interested in Visual Basic programming. Although every effort and care has been taken to make the information as accurate as possible, the author shall not be liable for any error, harm or damage arising from using the instructions given in this book.

About the Author

Dr. Liew Voon Kiong holds a bachelor's degree in Mathematics, a master's degree in Management and a doctorate in Business Administration. He has been involved in Visual Basic programming for more than 20 years. He created the popular online Visual Basic Tutorial at www.vbtutor.net, which has attracted millions of visitors since 1996. It has consistently been one of the highest ranked Visual Basic websites.

To provide more support for Visual Basic students, teachers, and hobbyists, Dr. Liew has written this book to complement the free Visual Basic 2017 tutorial with much more content. He is also the author of the Visual Basic Made Easy series, which includes **Visual Basic 6 Made Easy, Visual Basic 2008 Made Easy, Visual Basic 2010 Made Easy, Visual Basic 2013 Made Easy** and **Excel VBA Made Easy.** Dr. Liew's books have been used in high school and university computer science courses all over the world.

Table of Contents

Games and Fun

1.1 Simple Animated Slot Machine

This simple slot machine was created using Visual Basic 6. While it does not exactly resemble the real machines played in casinos, it does demonstrate the concept of randomness and probability in an actual slot machine. Slot machine is a game of chance; many different outcomes will appear when the player presses the play button.

In this program, you need to draw an array of nine shapes ,Visual Basic will automatically label the shapes as shape1(0), shape1(1), shape1(2), shape1(3), shape1(4), shape1(5), shape1(6), shape1(7) and shape1(8) respectively. Arrange the shapes into three rows. Write the code so that only three types of shapes appear randomly. The shapes are square, oval and rectangle. Their appearance can be set at runtime using the Shape properties. For example, Shape1 (0).Shape=0 means it is a rectangle, Shape1 (0).Shape=1 is a square and Shape1 (0).Shape=2 is an oval shape. The colors of the shapes are controlled by the **FillColor** property of the shapes. For example, Shape1 (0).**FillColor=vbRed** will give the shape a red color. Besides, the default FillStyle property is transparent; therefore you need to set the FillStyle property to solid so that the colors can show up.

Randomness can be achieved by using the **RND** function. You also need to insert a timer to create the animated effect of the slot machine. The time interval is set to 10 so that the shapes change at a fast rate thus creates the illusion of animation. The program also uses a variable x to control the timer so that it can be stopped when x achieve certain value, otherwise the program will loop forever.

The Design Interface

The Runtime Interface

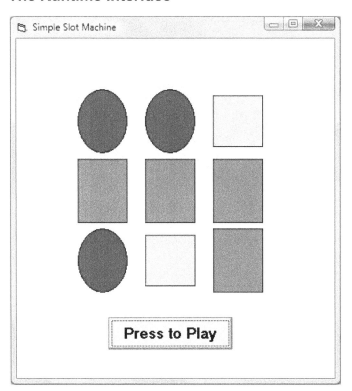

The code

```
Private Sub Command1_Click()
'To start the timer
Timer1.Enabled = True
x = 0
End Sub
Private Sub Timer1_Timer()
x = x + 10
Dim a, i As Integer
For i = 0 To 8
'To generate random integers 0,1 and 2
a = Int(Rnd * 3)
Shape1(i).Shape = a
Shape1(i).FillStyle = Solid
If a = 0 Then
Shape1(i).FillColor = vbRed
ElseIf a = 1 Then
Shape1(i).FillColor = vbGreen
Else
Shape1(i).FillColor = vbBlue
End If
Next i
'To stop the timer
If x > 500 Then
Timer1.Enabled = False
End If

End Sub
```

1.2 Advanced Animated Slot Machine

This is a more advanced animated slot machine created using Visual Basic 6. This is an improvement from the simple animated slot machine as the player can enter the amount to bet. Besides that, you can add sound and music to the program. The interface is shown below:

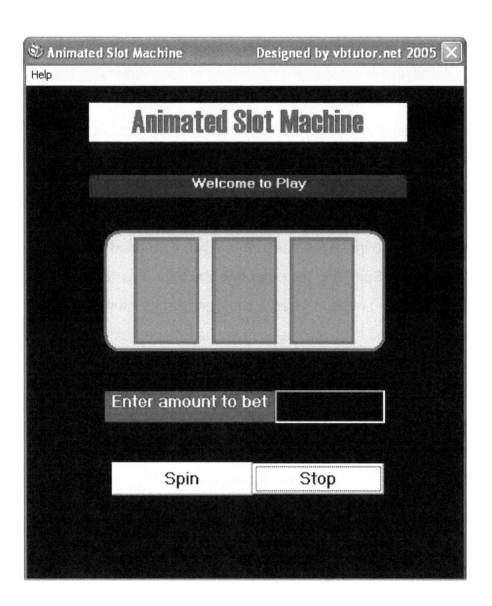

To design the interface, drag the form to a suitable size. Insert a label control and place it at the top part of the part. Change its caption to 'Animated Slot Machine', set proper font type, font size as well as foreground and background colors. Insert another label control and place it immediately below the first label. This label serves as display panel for showing how much the user has won. The display here will be animated. Next, place a shape control and set its shape property to rounded rectangle. Drag it to a proper size and fill it with a suitable solid color. It will act as the background panel for the spinning shapes. Now for the spinning shapes, insert a shape control into the form and then copy and paste repeatedly to create a control array of three shapes, each will be differentiated by its index , the first is shape1(0), the second is shape1(1) and the third shape1(2). Retain the default shape property as rectangle and change their shapes during runtime. Place all the three shapes on top of the first shape control, use color to make the former shapes stand out. Insert another label below the shape controls above and change its caption to "Enter amount to bet" to give instruction to the player the amount they want to bet. In order to let the player enters the amount they want to bet, insert a text box on the right of the above label and clear its text.

The next two controls you need to insert into the form are two command buttons, one of them you label its caption as "Spin" and the other one you label it as "Stop". To create the animated effect, you need to insert a timer and set its interval to 20, which is equivalent to 0.02 second. You also need to set its Enabled property as False so that the slot machine will not start until the user presses the "Spin" button. Besides, you need to insert the Multimedia Control to produce the sound effects. In order to include the multimedia control as one of the controls, click on project on the menu in Visual Basic 6 IDE and select components, and then click on **Microsoft Multimedia Control 6.0** to make it appear in the tool box. Now you can drag the Multimedia Control into your form. In this program, you need to use two Microsoft Multimedia Controls, one for playing the spinning sound and the other for the jackpot sound. Set the Visible property of both Microsoft Multimedia Controls as False so that the user will not see them at runtime. Lastly, insert a menu item and label it as "Help" and a submenu item and label it as "Instruction"

The code

```
Dim x As Integer
Dim amount As Integer
Dim a, b, c As Integer

Private Sub Spin_Click()
Timer1.Enabled = True
MMControl1.Command = "Close"
MMControl2.Command = "close"
x = 0
Label2.Caption = "Your Credits"
amount = Val(Text1)
End Sub

Private Sub Stop_Click()
Unload Me
End Sub

Private Sub Form_Click()
Label3.Visible = False
End Sub

Private Sub Form_Load()
Label1.Caption = " Welcome to Play"
Label3.Visible = False
End Sub

'To display instructions when the user clicks on the menu item
Help
Private Sub instruct_click()
 Label3.Visible = True
End Sub
```

```vb
Private Sub Text1_Change()
amount = Val(Text1)
End Sub


Private Sub Timer1_Timer()


If x < 500 Then
spin
Else
Timer1.Enabled = False
MMControl1.Command = "Stop"
Label1.Alignment = 2
If (a = 3 And b = 3 And c <> 3) Or (a = 3 And c = 3 And b <> 3)Or_
 (b = 3 And c = 3 And a <> 3) Then
Label1.Caption = " You win 20 dollars"
amount = amount + 20
End If


If (a = 4 And b = 4 And c <> 4) Or (a = 4 And c = 4 And b <> 4)Or_
(b = 4 And c = 4 And a <> 4) Then
Label1.Caption = " You win 30 dollars"
amount = amount + 30
End If


If (a = 5 And b = 5 And c <> 5) Or (a = 5 And c = 5 And b <> 5)Or_
 (b = 5 And c = 5 And a <> 5) Then
Label1.Caption = " You win 40 dollars"
amount = amount + 40
End If


If (a = 3 And b = 3 And c = 3) Or (a = 4 And b = 4 And c = 4) Or _
 (a = 5 And b = 5 And c = 5) Then
'To play sound
MMControl2.Notify = False
MMControl2.Wait = True
MMControl2.Shareable = False
MMControl2.DeviceType = "WaveAudio"
MMControl2.FileName = "C:\ My Documents\VB
program\audio\jackpot.wav"
MMControl2.Command = "Open"
MMControl2.Command = "Play"
```

```
Label1.Caption = "Congratulation! Jackpot!!! You win 200 dollars!"
amount = amount + 200
End If
If (a = 3 And b = 4 And c = 5) Or (a = 3 And b = 5 And c = 4) _
Or (a = 4 And b = 3 And c = 5) Or (a = 4 And b = 5 And c = 3) _
Or (a = 5 And b = 4 And c = 3) Or (a = 5 And b = 3 And c = 4) Then
Label1.Caption = "Too bad, you lost 50 dollars"
amount = amount - 50
End If


If amount < 0 Then
Label1.Caption = "Oh! You're bankrupt!"
End If
Text1.Text = Str$(amount)
End If
End Sub


'To simulate spinning of the shapes
Sub spin()
x = x + 10
Randomize Timer
a = 3 + Int(Rnd * 3)
b = 3 + Int(Rnd * 3)
c = 3 + Int(Rnd * 3)

MMControl1.Notify = False
MMControl1.Wait = True
MMControl1.Shareable = False
MMControl1.DeviceType = "WaveAudio"
MMControl1.FileName = "C:\ My Documents\VB
program\audio\slot2.wav"
MMControl1.Command = "Open"
MMControl1.Command = "Play"


Label1.Caption = "Good Luck!"
Label1.Alignment = a - 3
Shape1(0).Shape = a
If a = 3 Then
Shape1(0).FillColor = &HFF00&
End If
If a = 4 Then
```

```
Shape1(0).FillColor = &HFF00FF
End If


If a = 5 Then
Shape1(0).FillColor = &HFF0000
End If


Shape1(1).Shape = b
If b = 3 Then
Shape1(1).FillColor = &HFF00&
End If
If b = 4 Then
Shape1(1).FillColor = &HFF00FF
End If


If b = 5 Then
Shape1(1).FillColor = &HFF0000
End If


Shape1(2).Shape = c
If c = 3 Then
Shape1(2).FillColor = &HFF00&
End If
If c = 4 Then
Shape1(2).FillColor = &HFF00FF
End If
If c = 5 Then
Shape1(2).FillColor = &HFF0000
End If

End Sub
```

1.3 Professional Casino Slot Machine

This a slot machine that resembles the real slot machines in the casinos. To create the project, you need to insert three image boxes into the form and write code so that they will display a set of three different pictures randomly when the user presses on the spin button. It involves a randomization process. Next, insert a timer and write relevant code to produce animated effects. In addition, you can also insert the **Microsoft Multimedia Control** so that it can play sounds that synchronize with the spinning of the slot machine as well as when the player hits the jackpot.

In the program, you need to declare three variables a, b and c that will be randomly assigned the values of, 2 and 3 using the RND function. Based on these three random numbers, three different images will be loaded into the three image boxes randomly using the **LoadPicture** method. Animated effects are created by entering the above procedure under the control of Timer1, which will call the **spin** procedure after every interval until it fulfills a certain condition. Sounds are also added using the Microsoft Multimedia Control to make the game more realistic and interesting. The amount won is controlled by the **If....Then** statements

It is important that you define the correct path for the LoadPicture method; otherwise the program will not be able to run. For example, our path is **C:\VB program\Images\grape.gif**, you need to create the necessary folders and have the necessary image file if you wish to copy the program directly. If you place the image file in a differently folder, you need to modify the path accordingly. For example, if your image file is in D:\VB program\Images\grape.gif, then you need to modify the LoadPicture method to **LoadPicture ("D:\VB program\Images\grape.gif")**.

The Interface

The code

```vb
Dim x As Integer
Dim amount As Variant
Dim balance As Variant
Dim a, b, c As Integer


Private Sub Command1_Click()
End
End Sub


'Code for the Bet on balance button
Private Sub betbal_Click()
Label13.Caption = Str$(Val(Label6.Caption) + Val(Label13.Caption))
Label6.Caption = ""
End Sub
'Code for Cash Out button
Private Sub Cashout_Click()
If Val(Label13.Caption) > 0 Then
balance = Val(Label6.Caption) + Val(Label13.Caption)
Label13.Caption = ""
Label6.Caption = Str$(balance)
Label1.Caption = "Please bet again"
Else
Label1.Caption = "Sorry, you have no money to cash out."
End If
End Sub
Private Sub Form_Click()
Label3.Visible = False
End Sub


Private Sub Form_Load()
Label1.Caption = " Welcome to Play"
Label3.Visible = False
Image1(0).Picture = LoadPicture("C:\My Documents\VB &_
program\Images\grape.gif")
Image1(1).Picture = LoadPicture("C:\My Documents\VB &_
program\Images\cherry.gif")
Image1(2).Picture = LoadPicture("C:\ My Documents\ VB &_
program\Images\orange.gif")
End Sub
```

```vb
'To show instruction on a label control
Private Sub instruct_click()
Label3.Visible = True
End Sub


Private Sub Label12_Click()
Label13.Caption = Str$(Val(Label13.Caption) + Val(Text2.Text))
Text2.Text = ""
End Sub
'The spin procedure
Private Sub spin_Click()
Timer1.Enabled = True
MMControl1.Command = "Close"
MMControl2.Command = "close"
x = 0
amount = Val(Text1)
balance = Val(Label6)
End Sub


'Code for the Spin button
Private Sub spining_Click()
If Val(Label13.Caption) > 0 Then
Timer1.Enabled = True
MMControl1.Command = "Close"
MMControl2.Command = "close"
x = 0
amount = Val(Label13.Caption)
balance = Val(Label6)
Else
Label1.Caption = "Sorry, you don't have money to play, add cash."
End If
End Sub
'To stop the game
Private Sub stop_Click()
End
End Sub



Private Sub Timer1_Timer()
'Call the spin procedure
spin
```

```
x = x + 20

If x > 500 Then
Timer1.Enabled = False
MMControl1.Command = "Stop"
Label1.Alignment = 2

If (a = 3 And b = 3 And c <> 3) Or (a = 3 And c = 3 And b <> 3)Or_
(b = 3 And c = 3 And a <> 3) Then
Label1.Caption = " You win 20 dollars"
amount = amount + 20
End If


If (a = 4 And b = 4 And c <> 4) Or (a = 4 And c = 4 And b <> 4)Or_
(b = 4 And c = 4 And a <> 4) Then
Label1.Caption = " You win 30 dollars"
amount = amount + 30
End If


If (a = 5 And b = 5 And c <> 5) Or (a = 5 And c = 5 And b <> 5)Or_
(b = 5 And c = 5 And a <> 5) Then
Label1.Caption = " You win 40 dollars"
amount = amount + 40
End If


If (a = 3 And b = 3 And c = 3) Or (a = 4 And b = 4 And c = 4) Or_
(a = 5 And b = 5 And c = 5) Then
'Playing sound
MMControl2.Notify = False
MMControl2.Wait = True
MMControl2.Shareable = False
MMControl2.DeviceType = "WaveAudio"
MMControl2.FileName = "C:\My Documents\VB _
program\audio\jackpot.wav"
MMControl2.Command = "Open"
MMControl2.Command = "Play"

Label1.Caption = "Congratulation! Jackpot!!! You win 200 dollars!"
amount = amount + 200
End If
```

```
If (a = 3 And b = 4 And c = 5) Or (a = 3 And b = 5 And c = 4) Or _
(a = 4 And b = 3 And c = 5) Or (a = 4 And b = 5 And c = 3) Or _
(a = 5 And b = 4 And c = 3) Or (a = 5 And b = 3 And c = 4) Then
Label1.Caption = " Too bad, you lost 100 dollars"
amount = amount - 100
End If


If amount < 0 Then
Label1.Caption = "Oh! You're bankrupt! Add cash to play!"
End If
Label13.Caption = Str$(amount)
End If
End Sub
'The spin sub procedure
Sub spin()
a = 3 + Int(Rnd * 3)
b = 3 + Int(Rnd * 3)
c = 3 + Int(Rnd * 3)


MMControl1.Notify = False
MMControl1.Wait = True
MMControl1.Shareable = False
MMControl1.DeviceType = "WaveAudio"
MMControl1.FileName = "C:\ My Documents\VBprogram\audio\slot2.wav"
MMControl1.Command = "Open"
MMControl1.Command = "Play"
Label1.Caption = "Good Luck!"
Label1.Alignment = a - 3


If a = 3 Then
Image1(0).Picture = LoadPicture("C:\ My Documents\VB _
program\Images\grape.gif")
End If
If a = 4 Then
Image1(0).Picture = LoadPicture("C:\ My Documents\VBprogram\ _
Images\cherry.gif")
End If
If a = 5 Then
Image1(0).Picture = LoadPicture("C:\My Documents\VBprogram\ _
Images  \orange.gif")
End If
```

```
If b = 3 Then
Image1(1).Picture = LoadPicture("C: \ My Documents\VBprogram\_
Images\grape.gif")
End If
If b = 4 Then
Image1(1).Picture = LoadPicture("C:\ :\ My Documents\VBprogram\ _
Images \cherry.gif")
End If
If b = 5 Then
Image1(1).Picture = LoadPicture("C:\ My Documents\VBprogram\_
 Images  \orange.gif")
End If

If c = 3 Then
Image1(2).Picture = LoadPicture("C:\ My Documents\VBprogram\_
Images grape.gif")
End If
If c = 4 Then
Image1(2).Picture = LoadPicture("C:\ My Documents\VBprogram\_
 Images \cherry.gif")
End If
If c = 5 Then
Image1(2).Picture = LoadPicture("C:\ :\ My Documents\VBprogram\ _
Images \orange.gif")
End If
End Sub
```

1.4 Dice

This program creates a die which can be used to play board games. It can also be incorporated into VB games that require a die. VB games that you can create in Visual Basic are step and ladder game, monopoly and more. First of all, you draw a rounded square in the project windows. Secondly, you need to draw an array of seven dots using the shape control. VB will automatically labeled them as shape1(0), shape1(1),shape1(2), shape1(3), shape1(4), shape1(5) and shape1(6). You can control the appearance of the dots using the random function RND. Each time the user click the 'Roll' button, he or she can see different combinations of dots.

The Interface

The Code

```
Private Sub Command1_Click()
n = Int(1 + Rnd * 6)
For i = 0 To 6
    Shape1(i).Visible = False
Next
If n = 1 Then
    Shape1(3).Visible = True
    Shape2.FillColor = &HC0C0C0
```

```
End If
If n = 2 Then
    Shape1(2).Visible = True
    Shape1(4).Visible = True
    Shape2.FillColor = &H8080FF
End If
If n = 3 Then
    Shape1(2).Visible = True
    Shape1(3).Visible = True
    Shape1(4).Visible = True
    Shape2.FillColor = &H80FF&
 End If
If n = 4 Then
    Shape1(0).Visible = True
    Shape1(2).Visible = True
    Shape1(4).Visible = True
    Shape1(6).Visible = True
    Shape2.FillColor = &HFFFF00
 End If
If n = 5 Then
    Shape1(0).Visible = True
    Shape1(2).Visible = True
    Shape1(3).Visible = True
    Shape1(4).Visible = True
    Shape1(6).Visible = True
    Shape2.FillColor = &HFFFF&
 End If


 If n = 6 Then
    Shape1(0).Visible = True
    Shape1(1).Visible = True
    Shape1(2).Visible = True
    Shape1(4).Visible = True
    Shape1(5).Visible = True
    Shape1(6).Visible = True
    Shape2.FillColor = &HFF00FF
 End If
End Sub
```

1.5 Jigsaw Puzzle

I guess everybody has played the jigsaw puzzle before, which is to fix the pieces of a picture that were cut into pieces and jumbled up. There are many levels of difficulties but eventually you can solve the puzzle. You can create a simple 3x3 jigsaw puzzle using Visual Basic 6. You can program it in such a way that you can drag and drop the pieces in the squares that you think are correct. If the piece is correct, it will stay in the correct square otherwise it will not stay there.

The interface

The code

```
Dim imgindex As Integer
Dim imgtag As String


Private Sub Image1_DragDrop(Index As Integer, Source As Control, X
As Single, _
Y As Single)
imgtag = Source.Tag
imgindex = Index
Select Case imgindex

Case 0
If imgtag = "11" Then
    Image1(0).Picture = Image1(9).Picture
    Source.Visible = False
Else
Source.Visible = True
End If

Case 1

If imgtag = "12" Then
    Image1(1).Picture = Image1(10).Picture
    Source.Visible = False
Else
Source.Visible = True
End If

Case 2

If imgtag = 13 Then
    Image1(2).Picture = Image1(11).Picture
    Source.Visible = False
Else
Source.Visible = True
End If

Case 3
```

```
If imgtag = 21 Then
     Image1(3).Picture = Image1(12).Picture
     Source.Visible = False
Else
Source.Visible = True
End If


Case 4

If imgtag = 22 Then
     Image1(4).Picture = Image1(13).Picture
     Source.Visible = False
Else
Source.Visible = True
End If


Case 5
If imgtag = 23 Then
     Image1(5).Picture = Image1(14).Picture
     Source.Visible = False
Else
Source.Visible = True
End If


Case 6
If imgtag = 31 Then
     Image1(6).Picture = Image1(15).Picture
     Source.Visible = False
Else
Source.Visible = True
End If

Case 7

If imgtag = 32 Then
     Image1(7).Picture = Image1(16).Picture
     Source.Visible = False
Else
Source.Visible = True
End If
```

```
Case 8

If imgtag = 33 Then
    Image1(8).Picture = Image1(17).Picture
    Source.Visible = False
Else
Source.Visible = True
End If
End Select

End Sub
```

1.6 Memory Game

This is a typical memory game for children. The user has to click the rectangles to reveal the hidden pictures and if two of the pictures are matched they will disappear. He or she wins the game when all the pictures are cleared.

In this program, you need to add an array of twelve image controls and twelve picture boxes to the form, and cover the images with the picture boxes. In order to match the images, you can use tags to identify them; same images should be given the same tags. The tags are being set at the images' properties windows. When two picture boxes covering the images is being clicked, the program checks for the tags of the images and if found that they are the same, then they become invisible.

The Interface

29

The code

```vb
Sub check()
'Check whether the images are the same or not
For i = 0 To 11
If Picture1(i).Visible = False Then
For j = 0 To 11
If Picture1(j).Visible = False Then
If i <> j And Image1(i).Tag = Image1(j).Tag Then
Image1(j).Visible = False
Image1(i).Visible = False
Picture1(j).Visible = False
Picture1(i).Visible = False
End If

If i <> j And Image1(i).Tag <> Image1(j).Tag And Image1(i).Visible
= True And _ Image1(j).Visible = True Then
Picture1(j).Visible = True
Picture1(i).Visible = True
End If
End If

Next j

End If

Next i

Timer1.Enabled = False
If Picture1(0).Visible = False _
And Picture1(1).Visible = False _
And Picture1(2).Visible = False _
And Picture1(3).Visible = False _
And Picture1(4).Visible = False _
And Picture1(5).Visible = False _
And Picture1(6).Visible = False _
And Picture1(7).Visible = False _
And Picture1(8).Visible = False _
And Picture1(9).Visible = False _
```

```vb
And Picture1(10).Visible = False _
And Picture1(11).Visible = False _
Then
MMControl1.Notify = False
MMControl1.Wait = True
MMControl1.Shareable = False
MMControl1.DeviceType = "WaveAudio"
MMControl1.FileName = "D:\Liew Folder\VB
program\audio\applause.wav"
MMControl1.Command = "Open"
MMControl1.Command = "Play"
End If

End Sub


Private Sub picture1_Click(Index As Integer)
Picture1(Index).Visible = False
Timer1.Enabled = True
End Sub

Private Sub Timer1_Timer()
check
End Sub
```

1.7 Passwords Cracking Program

This passwords cracking program can generate possible passwords and compares each of them with the actual password; and if the generated password found to be equal to the actual password, login will be successful.

The Interface

In this program, you need to add three timers to the form. Next, enter the passwords generating code under each of the Timer ( ) event by double-clicking the relevant timer. The interval of the timers can be set in their properties window where a value of 1 is equivalent to 1 millisecond, and a value of 1000 is 1 second; the smaller the value, the shorter the interval. The Timer's Enabled property is set to false so that the program will only start generating the passwords after the user clicks on the command button.

You can generate random passwords by using the **Rnd** function. **Rnd** is a Visual Basic function that generates a random number between 0 and 1. **Int** is a Visual

Basic function that returns an integer by ignoring the decimal part of that number. For example, Int(Rnd * 255) returns an integer between 0 and 255.

This program only deals with three-character passwords so as to make the code simpler so that every reader can grasp the concept easily. In order to generate the alphanumeric characters, you can use the **Chr** function. The Chr function returns the string that corresponds to an ASCII code. For example, Chr(65)=A and Chr(37)=%. There are altogether 255 characters. The program needs to generate the characters for each of the characters in the passwords and compare them with the corresponding character in the password entered by the user. To achieve the purpose, you need to declare three integers, namely code1, code2 and code 3 respectively. Each of the aforementioned integers will generate ASCII codes between 0 and 255 using the syntax

```
code1 = Int(Rnd * 255)
code2 = Int(Rnd * 255)
code3 = Int(Rnd * 255)
```

Besides that, you also need to declare three strings; they are p1 to denote the first character of the password, p2 to denote the second character of the password and p3 to denote the third character of the password. You can then use the **Chr** function to find the corresponding alphanumeric character from randomly generated ASCII codes using the following syntax:

```
p1 = Chr(code1)
p2 = Chr(code2)
p3 = Chr(code1)
```

After generating the characters, the program compares them to the characters of the actual password using the following syntax:

```
If Chr(code1) = Left(password, 1) Then
    p1 = Chr(code1)
If Chr(code2) = Mid(password, 2, 1) Then
p2 = Chr(code2)
If Chr(code3) = Right(password, 1) Then
    p3 = Chr(code3)
```

Finally, the program uses If…Then…Else to check whether the generated password is equal the actual password or not using the following syntax:

```
Text1.Text = p1 & p2 & p3
```

If they are equal, the passwords generating process will be terminated by setting the Timer1.Enabled property to false.

The Code

```
Dim password As String * 3
Dim crackpass As String
Dim p1, p2, p3 As String
Dim code1, code2, code3 As Integer
Dim x As Integer

Sub checkstatus()

Text1.Text = p1 & p2 & p3
If Text1.Text = password Then
Label1.Visible = True
Label1.Caption = "Password Cracked!  Login Successful!"
Else
Text1.Text = Chr(code1) + Chr(code2) + Chr(code3)
Label1.Visible = True
Label1.Caption = "Generating passwords, please wait...."
End If
End Sub
```

```vb
Private Sub Command1_Click()
Timer1.Enabled = True
Timer2.Enabled = True
Timer3.Enabled = True

End Sub

Private Sub Command2_Click()
Text2.Visible = False
Label2.Visible = False
Command2.Visible = False
password = Text2.Text
End Sub

Private Sub Command3_Click()
Label1.Visible = False
Text2.Visible = True
Label2.Visible = True
Command2.Visible = True
Text2.Text = ""
Text1.Text = ""
End Sub

Private Sub Command4_Click()
Timer1.Enabled = False
Timer2.Enabled = False
Timer3.Enabled = False
Text1.Text = ""
Label1.Caption = "Please try again"
End Sub

Private Sub Command5_Click()
End
End Sub

Private Sub Timer1_Timer()
 code1 = Int(Rnd * 255)

If Chr(code1) = Left(password, 1) Then
    p1 = Chr(code1)
```

```
Timer1.Enabled = False
Else
checkstatus
End If
checkstatus

End Sub


Private Sub Timer2_Timer()
code2 = Int(Rnd * 255)
If Chr(code2) = Mid(password, 2, 1) Then
    p2 = Chr(code2)
Timer2.Enabled = False
Else
checkstatus
End If
checkstatus
End Sub


Private Sub Timer3_Timer()

 code3 = Int(Rnd * 255)
If Chr(code3) = Right(password, 1) Then
    p3 = Chr(code3)
Timer3.Enabled = False
Else
checkstatus

End If
 checkstatus

End Sub
```

1.8 Reversi

This is the mini version of the typical reversi game. The program uses two sets of two-dimensional arrays (4x4) and declare them as Boolean , one represent the white pieces and the other one represent the black pieces. If a white piece or a black piece occupies a square, the variable becomes true, otherwise it is false.

By using this concept, the program can check how many white and black pieces appear on the reversi board and which positions they occupy. The program uses If...Then and Select Case.... End Select statements to check for conditions whether a white piece or a black piece can be put in a certain position so that the pieces trapped in between will change color. You can also add a procedure to display the number of white pieces and the number of black pieces at any one time and also the name of the winner.

To design the interface, you need to insert an image control and then copy and paste the image repeatedly to form a 4x4 array of images. Each image is defined by its index. For example, Image1 (0) is the first image Image1 (1) is the second image, Image1(2) is the third image and so on. The positions of the images are shown in the diagram below:

Image1(12)	Image1(13)	Image1(14)	Image1(15)
Image1(8)	Image1(9)	Image1(10)	Image1(11)
Image1(4)	Image1(5)	Image1(6)	Image1(7)
Image1(0)	Image1(1)	Image1(2)	Image1(3)

Next you need to create two images, a white solid circle and a black solid circle, save them as jpeg files. Load them into two image controls on the form. You can use whatever name for the two images, we used image17 to denote the while solid circle and image18 to denote the black circle. The two images are very important as you will later use the **dragdrop** method to enable the user to drag and drop the images into the circles:

The Interface

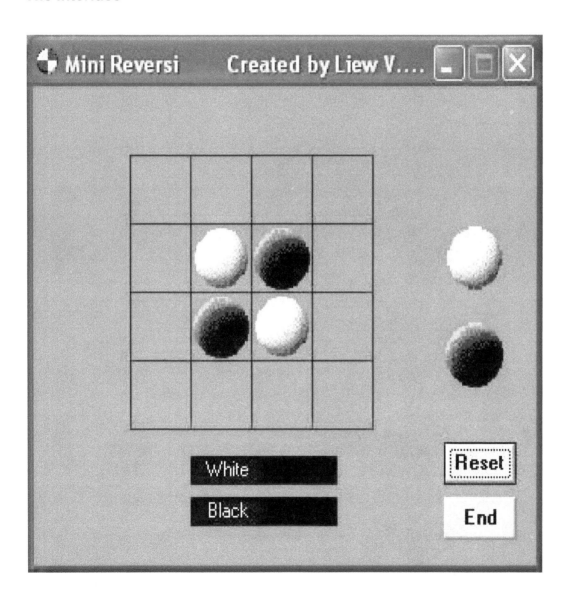

The Code

```vb
Option Base 1
Dim white(4, 4) As Boolean
Dim black(4, 4) As Boolean
Dim i, j, k, w, b As Integer
Dim imgtag As String


Private Sub Command1_Click()
'To reset the game
Label3.Caption = ""
Label4.Caption = ""
Label5.Visible = False


For m = 0 To 15
Image1(m).Picture = LoadPicture("")
Next m
Image1(5).Picture = Image18.Picture
Image1(10).Picture = Image18.Picture
Image1(9).Picture = Image17.Picture
Image1(6).Picture = Image17.Picture
Checkstatus
End Sub

Private Sub Command2_Click()
End
End Sub

Private Sub Form_Load()
Label5.Visible = False
Image1(5).Picture = Image18.Picture
Image1(10).Picture = Image18.Picture
Image1(9).Picture = Image17.Picture
Image1(6).Picture = Image17.Picture
End Sub
```

```vb
Private Sub Image1_DragDrop(Index As Integer, Source As Control, X
As Single, Y As Single)
imgtag = Source.Tag
checkstatus

'To  check whether image1(0)is destination of dragdrop and make
sure it is empty
If Index = 0 And black(1, 1) = False And white(1, 1) = False Then
Select Case imgtag
Case "white"
'Check row

If black(2, 1) = True And white(3, 1) = True Then
Image1(0).Picture = Image17.Picture
Image1(1).Picture = Image17.Picture

End If

If black(2, 1) = True And black(3, 1) = True And white(4, 1)= True
Then
Image1(0).Picture = Image17.Picture
Image1(1).Picture = Image17.Picture
Image1(2).Picture = Image17.Picture

End If
'check diagonal

If black(2, 2) = True And white(3, 3) = True Then
Image1(0).Picture = Image17.Picture
Image1(5).Picture = Image17.Picture
End If

If black(2, 2) = True And black(3, 3) = True And white(4, 4)= True
Then
Image1(0).Picture = Image17.Picture
Image1(5).Picture = Image17.Picture
Image1(10).Picture = Image17.Picture
End If
'Check column
If black(1, 2) = True And white(1, 3) = True Then
```

```
Image1(0).Picture = Image17.Picture
Image1(4).Picture = Image17.Picture
End If
If black(1, 2) = True And black(1, 3) = True And white(1, 4) =True
Then
Image1(0).Picture = Image17.Picture
Image1(4).Picture = Image17.Picture
Image1(8).Picture = Image17.Picture
End If


Case "black"
If white(2, 1) = True And black(3, 1) = True Then
Image1(0).Picture = Image18.Picture
Image1(1).Picture = Image18.Picture


End If


If white(2, 1) = True And white(3, 1) = True And black(4, 1)= True
Then
Image1(0).Picture = Image18.Picture
Image1(1).Picture = Image18.Picture
Image1(2).Picture = Image18.Picture


End If


If white(2, 2) = True And black(3, 3) = True Then
Image1(0).Picture = Image18.Picture
Image1(5).Picture = Image18.Picture
End If


If white(2, 2) = True And white(3, 3) = True And black(4, 4)= True
Then
Image1(0).Picture = Image18.Picture
Image1(5).Picture = Image18.Picture
Image1(10).Picture = Image18.Picture
End If
'Check column
If white(1, 2) = True And black(1, 3) = True Then
Image1(0).Picture = Image17.Picture
Image1(4).Picture = Image17.Picture
End If
```

```vb
If white(1, 2) = True And white(1, 3) = True And black(1, 4)= True
Then
Image1(0).Picture = Image17.Picture
Image1(4).Picture = Image17.Picture
Image1(8).Picture = Image17.Picture
End If
End Select
End If


'To compute the probabilities for position (2,1)

If Index = 1 And black(2, 1) = False And white(2, 1) = False Then
checkstatus
Select Case imgtag
Case "white"

If black(3, 1) = True And white(4, 1) = True Then
Image1(1).Picture = Image17.Picture
Image1(2).Picture = Image17.Picture
End If


If black(3, 2) = True And white(4, 3) = True Then
Image1(1).Picture = Image17.Picture
Image1(6).Picture = Image17.Picture
End If


If black(2, 2) = True And white(2, 3) = True Then
Image1(1).Picture = Image17.Picture
Image1(5).Picture = Image17.Picture
End If


If black(2, 2) = True And black(2, 3) = True And white(2, 4)= True
Then
Image1(1).Picture = Image17.Picture
Image1(5).Picture = Image17.Picture
Image1(9).Picture = Image17.Picture
End If


Case "black"
```

```
If white(3, 1) = True And black(4, 1) = True Then
Image1(1).Picture = Image18.Picture
Image1(2).Picture = Image18.Picture
End If


If white(3, 2) = True And black(4, 3) = True Then
Image1(1).Picture = Image18.Picture
Image1(6).Picture = Image18.Picture
End If


If white(2, 2) = True And black(2, 3) = True Then
Image1(1).Picture = Image18.Picture
Image1(5).Picture = Image18.Picture
End If


If white(2, 2) = True And white(2, 3) = True And black(2, 4) =
True Then
Image1(1).Picture = Image18.Picture
Image1(5).Picture = Image18.Picture
Image1(9).Picture = Image18.Picture
End If

End Select

End If


'To compute the position for (3,1)

If Index = 2 And black(3, 1) = False And white(3, 1) = False Then
Select Case imgtag
Case "white"

If black(2, 1) = True And white(1, 1) = True Then
Image1(1).Picture = Image17.Picture
Image1(2).Picture = Image17.Picture
End If


If black(2, 2) = True And white(1, 3) = True Then
Image1(2).Picture = Image17.Picture
```

```
Image1(5).Picture = Image17.Picture
End If
If black(3, 2) = True And white(3, 3) = True Then
Image1(2).Picture = Image17.Picture
Image1(6).Picture = Image17.Picture
End If


If black(3, 2) = True And black(3, 3) = True And white(3, 4) =
True Then
Image1(2).Picture = Image17.Picture
Image1(6).Picture = Image17.Picture
Image1(10).Picture = Image17.Picture
End If


Case "black"

If white(2, 1) = True And black(1, 1) = True Then
Image1(1).Picture = Image18.Picture
Image1(2).Picture = Image18.Picture
End If


If white(2, 2) = True And black(1, 3) = True Then
Image1(2).Picture = Image18.Picture
Image1(5).Picture = Image18.Picture
End If


If white(3, 2) = True And black(3, 3) = True Then
Image1(2).Picture = Image18.Picture
Image1(6).Picture = Image18.Picture
End If


If white(3, 2) = True And white(3, 3) = True And black(3, 4) =
True Then
Image1(2).Picture = Image18.Picture
Image1(6).Picture = Image18.Picture
Image1(10).Picture = Image18.Picture
End If


End Select


End If
```

```vb
'To compute position (4,1)

If Index = 3 And black(4, 1) = False And white(4, 1) = False Then
Select Case imgtag
Case "white"

If black(3, 1) = True And white(2, 1) = True Then
Image1(2).Picture = Image17.Picture
Image1(3).Picture = Image17.Picture
End If

If black(3, 1) = True And black(2, 1) = True And white(1, 1) =
True Then
Image1(1).Picture = Image17.Picture
Image1(2).Picture = Image17.Picture
Image1(3).Picture = Image17.Picture
End If

If black(3, 2) = True And white(2, 3) = True Then
Image1(3).Picture = Image17.Picture
Image1(6).Picture = Image17.Picture
End If

If black(3, 2) = True And black(2, 3) = True And white(1, 4) =
True Then
Image1(3).Picture = Image17.Picture
Image1(6).Picture = Image17.Picture
Image1(9).Picture = Image17.Picture
End If

If black(4, 2) = True And white(4, 3) = True Then
Image1(3).Picture = Image17.Picture
Image1(7).Picture = Image17.Picture
End If

If black(4, 2) = True And black(4, 3) = True And white(4, 4) =
True Then
Image1(3).Picture = Image17.Picture
Image1(7).Picture = Image17.Picture
```

```
Image1(11).Picture = Image17.Picture
End If
Case "black"


If white(3, 1) = True And black(2, 1) = True Then
Image1(2).Picture = Image18.Picture
Image1(3).Picture = Image18.Picture
End If


If white(3, 1) = True And white(2, 1) = True And black(1, 1) =
True Then
Image1(1).Picture = Image18.Picture
Image1(2).Picture = Image18.Picture
Image1(3).Picture = Image18.Picture
End If



If white(3, 2) = True And black(2, 3) = True Then
Image1(3).Picture = Image18.Picture
Image1(6).Picture = Image18.Picture
End If


If white(4, 2) = True And black(4, 3) = True Then
Image1(3).Picture = Image18.Picture
Image1(7).Picture = Image18.Picture
End If


If white(4, 2) = True And white(4, 3) = True And black(4, 4) =
True Then
Image1(3).Picture = Image18.Picture
Image1(7).Picture = Image18.Picture
Image1(11).Picture = Image18.Picture
End If


If white(3, 2) = True And white(2, 3) = True And black(1, 4) =
True Then
Image1(3).Picture = Image18.Picture
Image1(6).Picture = Image18.Picture
Image1(9).Picture = Image18.Picture
End If
```

```
End Select

End If

'To compute position (1,2)

If Index = 4 And black(1, 2) = False And white(1, 2) = False Then
Select Case imgtag
Case "white"

'Check row
If black(2, 2) = True And white(3, 2) = True Then
Image1(4).Picture = Image17.Picture
Image1(5).Picture = Image17.Picture
End If

If black(2, 2) = True And black(3, 2) = True And white(4, 2) =
True Then
Image1(4).Picture = Image17.Picture
Image1(5).Picture = Image17.Picture
Image1(6).Picture = Image17.Picture
End If

'check column
If black(1, 3) = True And white(1, 4) = True Then
Image1(4).Picture = Image17.Picture
Image1(8).Picture = Image17.Picture
End If

'check diagonal
If black(2, 3) = True And white(3, 4) = True Then
Image1(4).Picture = Image17.Picture
Image1(9).Picture = Image17.Picture
End If

Case "black"

If white(2, 2) = True And black(3, 2) = True _
And black(2, 2) = False And white(3, 2) = False Then
Image1(4).Picture = Image18.Picture
Image1(5).Picture = Image18.Picture
```

```
End If


If white(2, 2) = True And white(3, 2) = True And black(4, 2) =
True Then
Image1(4).Picture = Image18.Picture
Image1(5).Picture = Image18.Picture
Image1(6).Picture = Image18.Picture
End If



If white(1, 3) = True And black(1, 4) = True Then
Image1(4).Picture = Image18.Picture
Image1(8).Picture = Image18.Picture
End If


If white(2, 3) = True And black(3, 4) = True _
And black(2, 3) = False And white(3, 4) = False Then
Image1(4).Picture = Image18.Picture
Image1(9).Picture = Image18.Picture
End If
End Select

End If


'To compute position (4,2)

If Index = 7 And black(4, 2) = False And white(4, 2) = False Then
Select Case imgtag
Case "white"

'Check row
If black(3, 2) = True And white(2, 2) = True Then
Image1(6).Picture = Image17.Picture
Image1(7).Picture = Image17.Picture
End If

If black(3, 2) = True And black(2, 2) = True And white(1, 2) =
True Then
Image1(5).Picture = Image17.Picture
Image1(6).Picture = Image17.Picture
Image1(7).Picture = Image17.Picture
```

```vb
End If

'check column
If black(4, 3) = True And white(4, 4) = True Then
Image1(7).Picture = Image17.Picture
Image1(11).Picture = Image17.Picture
End If

'check diagonal
If black(3, 3) = True And white(2, 4) = True Then
Image1(7).Picture = Image17.Picture
Image1(10).Picture = Image17.Picture

End If

Case "black"

If white(3, 2) = True And black(2, 2) = True Then
Image1(6).Picture = Image18.Picture
Image1(7).Picture = Image18.Picture
End If

If white(2, 2) = True And white(3, 2) = True And black(1, 2) =
True Then
Image1(5).Picture = Image18.Picture
Image1(6).Picture = Image18.Picture
Image1(7).Picture = Image18.Picture
End If

If white(4, 3) = True And black(4, 4) = True Then
Image1(7).Picture = Image18.Picture
Image1(11).Picture = Image18.Picture
End If

If white(3, 3) = True And black(2, 4) = True Then
Image1(7).Picture = Image18.Picture
Image1(10).Picture = Image18.Picture
End If

End Select
```

```
End If
'To compute position (1,3)


If Index = 8 And black(1, 3) = False And white(1, 3) = False Then
Select Case imgtag
Case "white"


'Check row
If black(2, 3) = True And white(3, 3) = True Then
Image1(8).Picture = Image17.Picture
Image1(9).Picture = Image17.Picture
End If


If black(2, 3) = True And black(3, 3) = True And white(4, 3) =
True Then
Image1(8).Picture = Image17.Picture
Image1(9).Picture = Image17.Picture
Image1(10).Picture = Image17.Picture
End If


'check column
If black(1, 2) = True And white(1, 1) = True Then
Image1(4).Picture = Image17.Picture
Image1(8).Picture = Image17.Picture
End If


'check diagonal
If black(2, 2) = True And white(3, 1) = True Then
Image1(5).Picture = Image17.Picture
Image1(8).Picture = Image17.Picture
End If


Case "black"


If white(2, 3) = True And black(3, 3) = True Then
Image1(8).Picture = Image18.Picture
Image1(9).Picture = Image18.Picture
End If


If white(2, 3) = True And white(3, 3) = True And black(4, 2) =
True Then
```

```
Image1(8).Picture = Image18.Picture
Image1(9).Picture = Image18.Picture
Image1(10).Picture = Image18.Picture
End If


If white(1, 2) = True And black(1, 1) = True Then
Image1(4).Picture = Image18.Picture
Image1(8).Picture = Image18.Picture
End If


If white(2, 2) = True And black(3, 1) = True Then
Image1(5).Picture = Image18.Picture
Image1(8).Picture = Image18.Picture
End If


End Select


End If



'To compute position (4,3)

If Index = 11 And black(4, 3) = False And white(4, 3) = False Then
Select Case imgtag
Case "white"

'Check Left
If black(3, 3) = True And white(2, 3) = True Then
Image1(10).Picture = Image17.Picture
Image1(11).Picture = Image17.Picture
End If

If black(3, 3) = True And black(2, 3) = True And white(1, 3) =
True Then
Image1(9).Picture = Image17.Picture
Image1(10).Picture = Image17.Picture
Image1(11).Picture = Image17.Picture
End If
```

```vb
'check column
If black(4, 2) = True And white(4, 1) = True Then
Image1(7).Picture = Image17.Picture
Image1(11).Picture = Image17.Picture
End If


'check diagonal
If black(3, 2) = True And white(2, 1) = True Then
Image1(6).Picture = Image17.Picture
Image1(11).Picture = Image17.Picture
End If


Case "black"

If white(3, 3) = True And black(2, 3) = True Then
Image1(10).Picture = Image18.Picture
Image1(11).Picture = Image18.Picture
End If


If white(3, 3) = True And white(2, 3) = True And black(1, 3) =
True Then
Image1(9).Picture = Image18.Picture
Image1(10).Picture = Image18.Picture
Image1(11).Picture = Image18.Picture
End If


If white(4, 2) = True And black(4, 1) = True Then
Image1(7).Picture = Image18.Picture
Image1(11).Picture = Image18.Picture
End If


If white(3, 2) = True And black(2, 1) = True Then
Image1(6).Picture = Image18.Picture
Image1(11).Picture = Image18.Picture
End If


End Select


End If
```

```
'To compute position (1,4)

If Index = 12 And black(1, 4) = False And white(1, 4) = False Then
Select Case imgtag
Case "white"

'Check row
If black(2, 4) = True And white(3, 4) = True Then
Image1(12).Picture = Image17.Picture
Image1(13).Picture = Image17.Picture
End If

If black(2, 4) = True And black(3, 4) = True And white(4, 4) =
True Then
Image1(12).Picture = Image17.Picture
Image1(13).Picture = Image17.Picture
Image1(14).Picture = Image17.Picture
End If

'check column
If black(1, 3) = True And white(1, 2) = True Then
Image1(8).Picture = Image17.Picture
Image1(12).Picture = Image17.Picture
End If

If black(1, 3) = True And black(1, 2) = True And white(1, 1) =
True Then
Image1(4).Picture = Image17.Picture
Image1(8).Picture = Image17.Picture
Image1(12).Picture = Image17.Picture
End If


'check diagonal
If black(2, 3) = True And white(3, 2) = True Then
Image1(9).Picture = Image17.Picture
Image1(12).Picture = Image17.Picture
End If
```

```vb
If black(2, 3) = True And black(3, 2) = True And white(4, 1) =
True Then
Image1(6).Picture = Image17.Picture
Image1(9).Picture = Image17.Picture
Image1(12).Picture = Image17.Picture
End If


Case "black"

'Check row
If white(2, 4) = True And black(3, 4) = True Then
Image1(12).Picture = Image18.Picture
Image1(13).Picture = Image18.Picture
End If


If white(2, 4) = True And white(3, 4) = True And black(4, 4) =
True Then
Image1(12).Picture = Image18.Picture
Image1(13).Picture = Image18.Picture
Image1(14).Picture = Image18.Picture
End If

'check column
If white(1, 3) = True And black(1, 2) = True Then
Image1(4).Picture = Image18.Picture
Image1(8).Picture = Image18.Picture
End If
If white(1, 3) = True And black(1, 2) = True And black(1, 1) =
True Then
Image1(4).Picture = Image18.Picture
Image1(8).Picture = Image18.Picture
Image1(12).Picture = Image18.Picture
End If

'check diagonal
If white(2, 3) = True And black(3, 2) = True Then
Image1(9).Picture = Image18.Picture
Image1(12).Picture = Image18.Picture
End If
```

```
If white(2, 3) = True And white(3, 2) = True And black(4, 1) =
True Then
Image1(6).Picture = Image18.Picture
Image1(9).Picture = Image18.Picture
Image1(12).Picture = Image18.Picture
End If
End Select

End If


'To compute position (2,4)


If Index = 13 And black(2, 4) = False And white(2, 4) = False Then
Select Case imgtag
Case "white"
'Check row
If black(3, 4) = True And white(4, 4) = True Then
Image1(13).Picture = Image17.Picture
Image1(14).Picture = Image17.Picture
End If


'check column
If black(2, 3) = True And white(2, 2) = True Then
Image1(9).Picture = Image17.Picture
Image1(13).Picture = Image17.Picture
End If


If black(2, 3) = True And black(2, 2) = True And white(2, 1) =
True Then
Image1(5).Picture = Image17.Picture
Image1(9).Picture = Image17.Picture
Image1(13).Picture = Image17.Picture
End If


'check diagonal
If black(3, 3) = True And white(4, 2) = True Then
Image1(10).Picture = Image17.Picture
Image1(13).Picture = Image17.Picture
End If


Case "black"
```

```
'Check row
If white(3, 4) = True And black(4, 4) = True Then
Image1(13).Picture = Image18.Picture
Image1(14).Picture = Image18.Picture
End If


'check column
If white(2, 3) = True And black(2, 2) = True Then
Image1(9).Picture = Image18.Picture
Image1(13).Picture = Image18.Picture
End If


If white(2, 3) = True And white(2, 2) = True And black(2, 1) =
True Then
Image1(5).Picture = Image18.Picture
Image1(9).Picture = Image18.Picture
Image1(13).Picture = Image18.Picture
End If


'check diagonal
If white(3, 3) = True And black(4, 2) = True Then
Image1(10).Picture = Image18.Picture
Image1(13).Picture = Image18.Picture
End If
End Select
End If


'To compute position (3,4)
If Index = 14 And black(3, 4) = False And white(3, 4) = False Then
Select Case imgtag
Case "white"


'Check row
If black(2, 4) = True And white(1, 4) = True Then
Image1(13).Picture = Image17.Picture
Image1(14).Picture = Image17.Picture
End If


'check column
If black(3, 3) = True And white(3, 2) = True Then
Image1(10).Picture = Image17.Picture
```

```vb
Image1(14).Picture = Image17.Picture
End If


If black(3, 3) = True And black(3, 2) = True And white(3, 1) =
True Then
Image1(6).Picture = Image17.Picture
Image1(10).Picture = Image17.Picture
Image1(14).Picture = Image17.Picture
End If


'check diagonal
If black(2, 3) = True And white(1, 2) = True Then
Image1(9).Picture = Image17.Picture
Image1(14).Picture = Image17.Picture
End If

Case "black"
'Check row
If white(2, 4) = True And black(1, 4) = True Then
Image1(13).Picture = Image18.Picture
Image1(14).Picture = Image18.Picture
End If


'check column
If white(3, 3) = True And black(3, 2) = True Then
Image1(10).Picture = Image18.Picture
Image1(14).Picture = Image18.Picture
End If


If white(3, 3) = True And white(3, 2) = True And black(3, 1) =
True Then
Image1(6).Picture = Image18.Picture
Image1(10).Picture = Image18.Picture
Image1(14).Picture = Image18.Picture
End If


'check diagonal
If white(2, 3) = True And black(1, 2) = True Then
Image1(9).Picture = Image18.Picture
Image1(14).Picture = Image18.Picture
End If
```

```
End Select
End If


'To compute position (4,4)


If Index = 15 And black(4, 4) = False And white(4, 4) = False Then
Select Case imgtag
Case "white"


'Check row
If black(3, 4) = True And white(2, 4) = True Then
Image1(14).Picture = Image17.Picture
Image1(15).Picture = Image17.Picture
End If
If black(3, 4) = True And black(2, 4) = True And white(1, 4) =
True Then
Image1(13).Picture = Image17.Picture
Image1(14).Picture = Image17.Picture
Image1(15).Picture = Image17.Picture
End If
'check column
If black(4, 3) = True And white(4, 2) = True Then
Image1(11).Picture = Image17.Picture
Image1(15).Picture = Image17.Picture
End If
If black(4, 3) = True And black(4, 2) = True And white(4, 1) =
True Then
Image1(7).Picture = Image17.Picture
Image1(11).Picture = Image17.Picture
Image1(15).Picture = Image17.Picture
End If
'check diagonal
If black(3, 3) = True And white(2, 2) = True Then
Image1(10).Picture = Image17.Picture
Image1(15).Picture = Image17.Picture
End If


If black(3, 3) = True And black(2, 2) = True And white(1, 1) =
True Then
Image1(5).Picture = Image17.Picture
Image1(10).Picture = Image17.Picture
```

```vb
Image1(15).Picture = Image17.Picture
End If


Case "black"
'Check row
If white(3, 4) = True And black(2, 4) = True Then
Image1(14).Picture = Image18.Picture
Image1(15).Picture = Image18.Picture
End If


If white(3, 4) = True And white(2, 4) = True And black(1, 4) =
True Then
Image1(13).Picture = Image18.Picture
Image1(14).Picture = Image18.Picture
Image1(15).Picture = Image18.Picture
End If


'check column
If white(4, 3) = True And black(4, 2) = True Then
Image1(11).Picture = Image18.Picture
Image1(15).Picture = Image18.Picture
End If


If white(4, 3) = True And white(4, 2) = True And black(4, 1) =
True Then
Image1(7).Picture = Image18.Picture
Image1(11).Picture = Image18.Picture
Image1(15).Picture = Image18.Picture
End If


'check diagonal
If white(3, 3) = True And black(2, 2) = True Then
Image1(10).Picture = Image18.Picture
Image1(15).Picture = Image18.Picture
End If


If white(3, 3) = True And white(2, 2) = True And black(1, 1) =
True Then
Image1(5).Picture = Image18.Picture
Image1(10).Picture = Image18.Picture
Image1(15).Picture = Image18.Picture
```

```
End If
End Select

End If
countcolor
If w + b = 16 Or b = 0 Or w = 0 Then
If w > b Then
Label5.Visible = True
Label5.Caption = " White Wins"
Else
Label5.Visible = True
Label5.Caption = "Black Wins"
End If

End If

End Sub

Sub checkstatus()
k = 0
For j = 1 To 4
For i = 1 To 4

If Image1(k).Picture = Image17.Picture Then
   white(i, j) = True

Else: white(i, j) = False
End If

If Image1(k).Picture = Image18.Picture Then
    black(i, j) = True
Else

black(i, j) = False

   End If
k = k + 1

Next i
Next j
End Sub
```

```
Sub countcolor()
k = 0
w = 0
b = 0


For j = 1 To 4
For i = 1 To 4


If Image1(k).Picture = Image17.Picture Then
   white(i, j) = True
   w = w + 1


   Else: white(i, j) = False
End If


If Image1(k).Picture = Image18.Picture Then
    black(i, j) = True
    b = b + 1
Else


black(i, j) = False


   End If
k = k + 1
Print n


Next i


Next j
Label3.Caption = Str$(w)
Label4.Caption = Str$(b)


End Sub
```

1.9 Snakes and Ladders Game

Snakes and Ladders game is a popular board game for young children. This game usually involves two or more players and they take turns to move by rolling a die. On the way to the finishing point, the players will encounter some obstacles in the form of snakes and some opportunities in the form of ladders. Whenever the player encounters a snake, or more accurately, the snake's head, he or she will be thrown back to an earlier position, which is at the snake's tail. On the other hand, whenever the player encounters a ladder, he or she can climb up the ladder to a higher position. The player who reaches the finishing point first wins the game

The Interface

To design the program, you need to use mathematical logics. Since the board comprises 10 rows and 10 columns, each box thus represents a cell with the relevant coordinates (column, row). Therefore, you need to define the coordinates of every cell by declaring two arrays row (10) and col (10) at the beginning of the procedure. To move the piece on the board, you can use the method **object.move col(i), row(j)**, where the program can initiate the values of col(i) and row(j) via a For....Next loop. As the motion is in a zigzag manner, you need to control the motion using reverse order and by imposing some conditions.

The first step in creating the game is to design the board using 100 label controls. The labels are numbered from 1 to 100. You shall fill these labels with different colors to give it a more appealing look. Next, insert various pictures of snakes using the image box and then draw the ladders using the line tool. In addition, you need to draw the die with the shape control, and add in the command buttons for rolling the die, starting a new game as well as exiting the game. Besides that, you need to insert two images to denote the players and then insert the label for the declaration of the winner. Lastly, insert two timers for animation purpose.

The initial part of the program is to declare various variables. The two most important variables are the arrays c (10) and r (10). The role of array r (10) is to denote the row numbers , where r(1)=row 1, r(2)=row 2 until r(10)=row 10. Similarly, c (10) is used to denote the column numbers, where c (1) =column 1, c (2) =column 2 until c (10) =column 10. After declaring the variables, you need to assign the coordinates of the center of all the boxes which can be denoted by (column, row) or (c (i), r (i)), using the procedure below:

```
Private Sub Form_Load ()
c (1) = 600
r(1) = 8200
For i = 1 To 9
c (i + 1) = c (i) + 800
```

```
Next
For j = 1 To 9
r (j + 1) = r (j) - 800
Next
End Sub
```

Next, you have to assign the initial position of the center of the first box (label) by looking at its distance from the left as well as from the top, and also its width, in the properties window. In this program, the distance of the first box from the left is 400 twips, and its width is 800 twips, therefore its center is 600 twips from the left. Using the statement c (i + 1) = c (i) + 800 within a For...Next loop, the distance between successive columns will be fixed at 800 twips. Similarly, the distance between rows can be determined using the same logic. The next most important step is to control the movement of the players' pieces. In order to do this, you have to use the variables totalnum and totalnum1 to denote the accumulated scores of the die for player 1 and player 2 respectively. For example, if the first score of the die is 3 and the second score of the die is 6 for player 1, then totalnum=9. You need to write the procedure for every row individually so that motion will be in a zigzag manner as shown in following figure.

←	←	←	←	←	←	←	←	←	←
→	→	→	→	→	→	→	→	→	↑
↑	←	←	←	←	←	←	←	←	←
→	→	→	→	→	→	→	→	→	↑
↑	←	←	←	←	←	←	←	←	←
→	→	→	→	→	→	→	→	→	↑
↑	←	←	←	←	←	←	←	←	←
→	→	→	→	→	→	→	→	→	↑
↑	←	←	←	←	←	←	←	←	←
→	→	→	→	→	→	→	→	→	↑

For the first row and for player 1, you can use the following procedure:

```
If player = 1 Then
totalnum = totalnum + num
If totalnum < 11 Then
Image1 (0).Move c (totalnum), r (1)
End If
```

Num is the score which appears on the die and totalnum is added to num to get the accumulated scores. In the first row, the number on the rightmost square is 10, which is equal to the number of columns across the first row. The statement

Image1 (0).Move c (totalnum), r (1) uses the Move method to move piece 1 (Image1(0)) across the column from left to right . For the movement in the second row, the direction is from right to left, so you need to use the following procedure:

```
If totalnum > 10 And totalnum < 21 Then
Image1 (0).Move c (21 - totalnum), r (2)
End If
```

The statement Image1 (0).Move c(21 - totalnum), r(2) will move Image1(0) from the position c(10),r(2) to c(1), r(2), i.e. from the square with number 11 to the square with number 20. The movement of the pieces for other positions follows the same logics. The procedure to move the pieces has to be placed under the Private Sub Timer1_Timer procedure (set the Timer1 interval to a certain value).

Before the program can work, you will need to write code for the die, which will determine how many steps the chess pieces will move. The interface of the die consists of 7 round shapes that are placed in a rounded square as shown in Figure 24.3. The seven round shapes are inserted as a control array with names starting with shape1 (0) to shape1 (6). The shape in the center is shape1 (3). The appearance of the round shapes are controlled by a randomization process that produce six random numbers using the statement num = Int(1 + Rnd * 6). For example, when num=1, only the round shape in the center appears while other round shapes are made invisible. Other combinations use the same logic

The Code

```
Option Base 1
Dim c (10) As Variant
Dim r (10) As Variant

 Dim x As Integer
 Dim m As Integer
 Dim n As Integer
 Dim num As Integer
 Dim totalnum As Single
 Dim totalnum1 As Single
 Dim player As Integer
 Dim t As Integer

Private Sub Command2_Click()
'To move the pieces to the original position
Image1 (0).Move 10200, 5520
Image1 (1).Move 10200, 6480
Totalnum = 0
totalnum1 = 0
Label2.Caption = ""
MMControl1.Command = "close"
End Sub

Private Sub Command3_Click ()
Unload Me
End Sub

Private Sub Form_Load ()
'To assign the column and row coordinates to all the boxes
c (1) = 600
r (1) = 8200
For i = 1 To 9
c (i + 1) = c (i) + 800
Next
```

```
For j = 1 To 9
r (j + 1) = r (j) - 800
Next
End Sub


'To roll the die
Private Sub roll ()
x = x + 10
Randomize Timer
num = Int(1 + Rnd * 6)
For i = 0 To 6
    Shape1 (i).Visible = False
Next
If num = 1 Then
    Shape1 (3).Visible = True
    Shape2.FillColor = &HC0C0C0

End If
If num = 2 Then
    Shape1 (2).Visible = True
    Shape1 (4).Visible = True
    Shape2.FillColor = &H8080FF
End If
If num = 3 Then
    Shape1 (2).Visible = True
    Shape1 (3).Visible = True
    Shape1 (4).Visible = True
    Shape2.FillColor = &H80FF&
 End If
If num = 4 Then
    Shape1 (0).Visible = True
    Shape1 (2).Visible = True
    Shape1 (4).Visible = True
    Shape1 (6).Visible = True
    Shape2.FillColor = &HFFFF00
 End If
If num = 5 Then
    Shape1 (0).Visible = True
    Shape1 (2).Visible = True
    Shape1 (3).Visible = True
    Shape1 (4).Visible = True
```

```vb
    Shape1 (6).Visible = True
    Shape2.FillColor = &HFFFF&
 End If


 If num = 6 Then
    Shape1 (0).Visible = True
    Shape1 (1).Visible = True
    Shape1 (2).Visible = True
    Shape1 (4).Visible = True
    Shape1 (5).Visible = True
    Shape1 (6).Visible = True
    Shape2.FillColor = &HFF00FF
 End If
End Sub


Private Sub Command1_Click (Index As Integer)
'To identify which player is clicking the roll die command
If Index = 0 Then
player = 1
End If


If Index = 1 Then
player = 2
End If
Timer1.Enabled = True
x = 0
End Sub


Private Sub Timer1_Timer ()
If x < 100 Then
Call roll
Else
Timer1.Enabled = False


'To move player 1 according to the total score of the die
'Movement across column 1 to column 10 and row 1 to row 10
If player = 1 Then
totalnum = totalnum + num
If totalnum < 11 Then
Image1 (0).Move c (totalnum), r (1)
If totalnum = 10 Then
```

```
Image1 (0).Move c (8), r (3)
totalnum = 28
End If
End If


If totalnum > 10 And totalnum < 21 Then
Image1 (0).Move c (21 - totalnum), r (2)
If totalnum = 17 Then
Image1 (0).Move c (4), r (4)
Totalnum = 37
End If
End If


If totalnum > 20 And totalnum < 31 Then
Image1 (0).Move c (totalnum - 20), r(3)
End If
If totalnum > 30 And totalnum < 41 Then
Image1 (0).Move c (41 - totalnum), r(4)
If totalnum = 34 Then
Image1 (0).Move c(5), r(2)
totalnum = 16
End If
If totalnum = 31 Then
Image1 (0).Move c (10), r (7)
totalnum = 70
End If
End If


If totalnum > 40 And totalnum < 51 Then
Image1 (0).Move c (totalnum - 40), r (5)
If totalnum = 45 Then
Image1 (0).Move c (4), r (9)
totalnum = 84
End If


If totalnum = 44 Then
Image1 (0).Move c(1), r(3)
totalnum = 21
End If
End If
```

```
If totalnum > 50 And totalnum < 61 Then
Image1 (0).Move c (61 - totalnum), r (6)
End If


If totalnum > 60 And totalnum < 71 Then
Image1 (0).Move c (totalnum - 60), r (7)
If totalnum = 68 Then
Image1 (0).Move c (8), r (5)
totalnum = 48
End If
End If


If totalnum > 70 And totalnum < 81 Then
Image1 (0).Move c (81 - totalnum), r (8)
If totalnum = 79 Then
Image1 (0).Move c (2), r (6)
totalnum = 59
End If
If totalnum = 78 Then
Image1 (0).Move c (4), r (10)
totalnum = 97
End If
End If


If totalnum > 80 And totalnum < 91 Then
Image1 (0).Move c (totalnum - 80), r (9)
End If
If totalnum > 90 And totalnum < 101 Then
Image1 (0).Move c (101 - totalnum), r (10)
If totalnum = 95 Then
Image1 (0).Move c(8), r(8)
totalnum = 73
End If
End If


If totalnum > 100 Or totalnum = 100 Then
Image1 (0).Move c (1), r(10)
End If
End If
```

```vbnet
'To move player 2 according to the total score of the die
 If player = 2 Then
 totalnum1 = totalnum1 + num
If totalnum1 < 11 Then
Image1 (1).Move c (totalnum1), r(1)
If totalnum1 = 10 Then
Image1 (1).Move c (8), r(3)
totalnum1 = 28
End If
End If
If totalnum1 > 10 And totalnum1 < 21 Then
Image1 (1).Move c (21 - totalnum1), r (2)
If totalnum1 = 17 Then
Image1 (1).Move c (4), r (4)
totalnum1 = 37
End If
End If
If totalnum1 > 20 And totalnum1 < 31 Then
Image1 (1).Move c (totalnum1 - 20), r(3)
End If
If totalnum1 > 30 And totalnum1 < 41 Then
Image1 (1).Move c (41 - totalnum1), r(4)
If totalnum1 = 34 Then
Image1 (1).Move c (5), r(2)
totalnum1 = 16
End If
If totalnum1 = 31 Then
Image1(1).Move c (10), r(7)
totalnum1 = 70
End If
If totalnum1 > 40 And totalnum1 < 51 Then
Image1(1).Move c(totalnum1 - 40), r(5)
If totalnum1 = 45 Then
Image1(1).Move c(4), r(9)
totalnum1 = 84
End If
If totalnum1 = 44 Then
Image1(1).Move c(1), r(3)
totalnum1 = 21
End If
End If
```

```
If totalnum1 > 50 And totalnum1 < 61 Then
Image1 (1).Move c (61 - totalnum1), r (6)
End If
If totalnum1 > 60 And totalnum1 < 71 Then
Image1 (1).Move c (totalnum1 - 60), r (7)
If totalnum1 = 68 Then
Image1 (1).Move c (8), r(5)
totalnum1 = 48
End If
End If
If totalnum1 > 70 And totalnum1 < 81 Then
Image1 (1).Move c (81 - totalnum1), r(8)
If totalnum1 = 79 Then
Image1 (1).Move c(2), r(6)
totalnum1 = 59
End If
If totalnum1 = 78 Then
Image1 (1).Move c (4), r (10)
totalnum1 = 97
End If
End If
If totalnum1 > 80 And totalnum1 < 91 Then
Image1 (1).Move c (totalnum1 - 80), r(9)
End If
If totalnum1 > 90 And totalnum1 < 101 Then
Image1 (1).Move c (101 - totalnum1), r (10)
If totalnum1 = 95 Then
Image1 (1).Move c (8), r (8)
totalnum1 = 73
End If
End If
If totalnum1 > 100 Or totalnum1 = 100 Then
Image1 (1).Move c (1), r (10)
End If
End If
'To play the applause sound when any one player reaches 100
If (totalnum > 100 Or totalnum = 100) And totalnum1 < 100 Then
Label2.Caption = "Player 1 Wins"
MMControl1.Notify = False
MMControl1.Wait = True
MMControl1.Shareable = False
```

```
MMControl1.DeviceType = "WaveAudio"
MMControl1.FileName = " D:\MyDocument\VB _
program\audio\applause.wav"
MMControl1.Command = "Open"
MMControl1.Command = "Play"
End If
If (totalnum1 > 100 Or totalnum1 = 100) And totalnum < 100 Then
Label2.Caption = "Player 2 Wins"
MMControl1.Notify = False
MMControl1.Wait = True
MMControl1.Shareable = False
MMControl1.DeviceType = "WaveAudio"
MMControl1.FileName = "D:\MyDocument\VB _
program\audio\applause.wav"
MMControl1.Command = "Open"
MMControl1.Command = "Play"
End If
End If
End Sub
```

1.10 Star War Game

The star war game is created using Visual Basic to demonstrate the principle of projectile, a typical physics problem. When a projectile is launched at a certain angle and with a certain initial velocity, the projectile can reach a certain range. The maximum range is at an angle of 45 degree. This principle can be applied in the military field where a missile can be launched at a certain velocity and angle in order to hit a remote target. It can also be applied in other scientific and technological fields. This game provides a good training for students in their abilities in making estimation.

The Interface

In this program, you can use the expression **v sin A - ½g t²** to represent the vertical component of the displacement and **v cos A** as the horizontal component of the displacement(where g is the gravitational acceleration , v the launch velocity and A the launch angle). To enable the missile to fly, you can use a combination of the **Object.Move** method and the object position's properties **object.left** and **Object.top**.

You also need to use randomize method so that the objects will appear at different positions randomly at each new game. In addition, you can use the randomize method to load different backgrounds at start up and at each new game.

The Code

```
Dim x As Variant
Dim a As Variant
Dim t As Variant
Dim y As Variant
Dim w As Variant
Dim i As Variant
Dim score As Integer
Dim left1, left2, left3, top1, top2, top3 As Variant
Dim backgr As Integer

Sub showfire()
Timer2.Enabled = True
End Sub

Sub reset()
'To move the missile to initial position
w = 0
Image1.Visible = True
Timer1.Enabled = False
Label4(0).Visible = False
Label4(1).Visible = False
Label4(2).Visible = False
Image1.Move 360, 6360
t = 0
End Sub
```

```vb
Private Sub Command1_Click()
Timer1.Enabled = True
End Sub


Private Sub Form_Click()
Label5.Visible = False
End Sub


Private Sub Form_Load()
left1 = Int(Rnd * 7000) + 1000
left2 = Int(Rnd * 7000) + 1000
left3 = Int(Rnd * 7000) + 1000
top1 = Int(Rnd * 5000) + 100
top2 = Int(Rnd * 5000) + 100
top3 = Int(Rnd * 5000) + 100
'To set the initial positions of the objects
Image2.Left = left1
Image3.Left = left2
Image4.Left = left3
Image2.Top = top1
Image3.Top = top2
Image4.Top = top3
w = 0
score = 0
Label7.Caption = Str(score)
End Sub


Private Sub Image7_Click()
Label5.Visible = False
End Sub


Private Sub Instruct_Click()
Label5.Visible = True
Label5.Caption = "To play the game, you need to key in the
velocity and the angle. The range of angle should be between 0 and
90 degree. After entering the above values, click launch to play.
After every trial, you have to reset the game. After striking all
the objects, press File menu and select new game to play again."
End Sub
```

```vb
Private Sub mnuExit_Click()
Unload Me
End Sub


Private Sub mnunew_Click()
w = 0
Randomize Timer
'To display all the objects again
left1 = Int(Rnd * 7000) + 1000
left2 = Int(Rnd * 7000) + 1000
left3 = Int(Rnd * 7000) + 1000
top1 = Int(Rnd * 5000) + 100
top2 = Int(Rnd * 5000) + 100
top3 = Int(Rnd * 5000) + 100
Image2.Left = left1
Image3.Left = left2
Image4.Left = left3
Image2.Top = top1
Image3.Top = top2
Image4.Top = top3
Image2.Visible = True
Image3.Visible = True
Image4.Visible = True
Image1.Visible = True
Timer1.Enabled = False
Label4(0).Visible = False
Label4(1).Visible = False
Label4(0).Visible = False
Label3.Caption = ""
Image1.Move 360, 6360
t = 0

End Sub


Private Sub Timer1_Timer()
MMControl1.Command = "close"
If Image1.Left < 15000 And Image1.Top < 9000 Then
v = Val(Text1.Text)
a = Val(Text2.Text)
t = t + 1
```

```vb
'use the projectile formula to move the missile  y=v(sinA)t
-1/2(g)sinA, x=v(cosA)t, A=Angle of launch
y = v * Sin(a * 3.141592654 / 180) * t - 4.9 * (t ^ 2)
x = v * Cos(a * 3.141592654 / 180) * t
Image1.Move Image1.Left + x, Image1.Top - y
If Image4.Visible = True And (Image1.Left < left3 + 240 And
Image1.Left > left3 - 240) And (Image1.Top < top3 + 240 And
Image1.Top > top3 - 240) Then
i = 2
Timer1.Enabled = False
showfire
Image4.Visible = False
Image1.Visible = False
'To trigger the sound
MMControl1.Notify = False
MMControl1.Wait = True
MMControl1.Shareable = False
MMControl1.DeviceType = "WaveAudio"
MMControl1.FileName = "C:\My Documents\VB program\audio\bomb.wav"
MMControl1.Command = "Open"
MMControl1.Command = "Play"
Label3.Caption = "You hit the satellite!"
Label4(2).Left = left3 + 240
Label4(2).Top = top3 + 240
Label4(2).Visible = True
Image5(2).Left = left3 + 240
Image5(2).Top = top3 + 240
score = score + 50
reset
ElseIf Image3.Visible = True And (Image1.Left < left2 + 240 And
Image1.Left > left2 - 240) And (Image1.Top < top2 + 240 And _
Image1.Top > top2 - 240) Then
Timer1.Enabled = False
i = 1
showfire
Image3.Visible = False
Image1.Visible = False
MMControl1.Notify = False
MMControl1.Wait = True
MMControl1.Shareable = False
MMControl1.DeviceType = "WaveAudio"
```

```vb
MMControl1.FileName = "C:\ My Documents\VB program\audio\bomb.wav"
MMControl1.Command = "Open"
MMControl1.Command = "Play"
Label3.Caption = "You hit the rocket!"
Label4(1).Left = left2 + 240
Label4(1).Top = top2 + 240
Label4(1).Visible = True
Image5(1).Left = left2 + 240
Image5(1).Top = top2 + 240
score = score + 100
reset
ElseIf Image2.Visible = True And (Image1.Left < left1 + 240 And _
Image1.Left > left1 - 240) And (Image1.Top < top1 + 240 And
Image1.Top > top1 - 240) Then
Timer1.Enabled = False
i = 0
showfire
Image2.Visible = False
Image1.Visible = False
MMControl1.Notify = False
MMControl1.Wait = True
MMControl1.Shareable = False
MMControl1.DeviceType = "WaveAudio"
MMControl1.FileName = "C:\ My Documents\VB program\audio\bomb.wav"
MMControl1.Command = "Open"
MMControl1.Command = "Play"
Label3.Caption = "You hit the Saturn!"
Label4(0).Left = left1 + 240
Label4(0).Top = top1 + 240
Label4(0).Visible = True
Image5(0).Left = left1 + 240
Image5(0).Top = top1 + 240
score = score + 200
reset
End If

Else
Label3.Caption = "You missed the target!"
Timer1.Enabled = False
reset
```

```
End If
'Show score
Label7.Caption = Str(score)
End Sub


Private Sub Timer2_Timer()
w = w + 1
If w < 30 Then
Image5(i).Visible = True
Label4(i).Visible = True
Else
Image5(i).Visible = False
Label4(i).Visible = False
Timer2.Enabled = False
End If
End Sub
```

1.11 Tic Tac Toe

Tic Tac Toe is a popular game which you can play anytime and anywhere as long as you have a piece of paper and pen, or you could draw it on sand or any surface. Now, let's program it in Visual Basic 6 so that you can play the game virtually.

To design the interface, first of all you need to draw four black straight lines on the form using the line control. Next, insert an image control then use copy and paste method to create nine image controls, Image1 (0) to Image1 (8) and arrange them in the following order:

Image1 (6)	Image1 (7)	Image1 (8)
Image1 (3)	Image1 (4)	Image1 (5)
Image1 (0)	Image1 (1)	Image1 (2)

In addition, you need to insert eight straight lines in red color that would cross out three crosses or three circles if they are aligned in a straight line side by side, as shown in the design interface. You need to make these lines invisible at start-up and make one of the lines appear whenever the above condition is fulfilled.

Finally, insert two pictures, one in the shape of a circle and the other one is in the shape of a cross to represent player 1 and player 2 respectively

The Design Interface

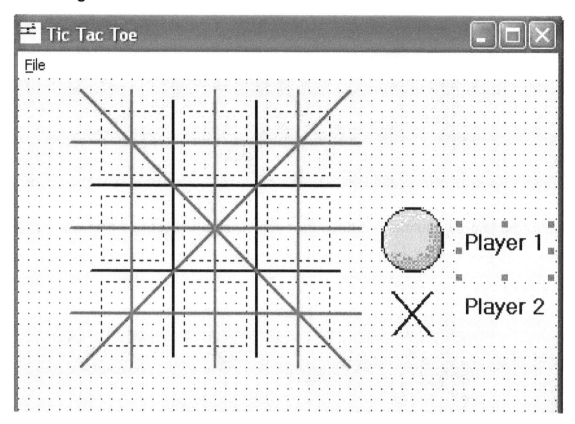

Now you need to write the code to make the game works. To check whether a position on the board is occupied or empty, you can create two arrays, **cross(8)** and **ball(8)** (you need to use ball instead of circle because circle is an internal function of VB) and declare them as Boolean. If **cross(n)=true**, it means position **n** is occupied by the player's piece which is a cross. On the other hand, **cross (n)=false** means position n is not occupied by a cross. It is the same for the **ball(n)** array. The value of n is the index of a particular image control. You need to create a subroutine **check_position** to check the position of the player's piece. The code is as follows:

```
Sub check_position()
For m = 0 To 8

If Image1(m).Picture = Image2.Picture Then
ball(m) = True
```

```
Else: ball(m) = False
End If


If Image1(m).Picture = Image3.Picture Then
cross(m) = True
Else
cross(m) = False
 End If
 Next
End Sub
```

Another important subroutine you need to create is **check_status .** This subroutine will check whether three similar shapes have appeared. Part of the subroutine is as follows:

```
Sub check_status()
If ball(0) = True And ball(1) = True And ball(2) = True Then
Line10.Visible = True
Player1_WinMsg
ElseIf ball(3) = True And ball(4) = True And ball(5) = True Then
Line9.Visible = True
Player1_WinMsg
ElseIf cross(0) = True And cross(1) = True And cross(2) = True
Then
Line10.Visible = True
Player2_WinMsg
ElseIf cross(3) = True And cross(4) = True And cross(5) = True
Then
Line9.Visible = True
Player2_WinMsg
End Sub
```

Both subroutines Player1_WinMsg and Player2_WinMsg are to display winning messages "Player1 win!" and "Player2 Win!" respectively.

The Code

```
Dim cross(8) As Boolean
```

```vb
Dim ball(8) As Boolean
Dim n, m As Integer
Dim player As Integer


'To check whether three similar images align in one straight line
side by side or not
Sub check_status()
If ball(0) = True And ball(1) = True And ball(2) = True Then
Line10.Visible = True
Player1_WinMsg
ElseIf ball(3) = True And ball(4) = True And ball(5) = True Then
Line9.Visible = True
Player1_WinMsg
ElseIf ball(6) = True And ball(7) = True And ball(8) = True Then
Line8.Visible = True
Player1_WinMsg
ElseIf ball(0) = True And ball(3) = True And ball(6) = True Then
Line5.Visible = True
Player1_WinMsg
ElseIf ball(1) = True And ball(4) = True And ball(7) = True Then
Line6.Visible = True
Player1_WinMsg
ElseIf ball(2) = True And ball(5) = True And ball(8) = True Then
Line7.Visible = True
Player1_WinMsg
ElseIf ball(0) = True And ball(4) = True And ball(8) = True Then
Line12.Visible = True
Player1_WinMsg
ElseIf ball(2) = True And ball(4) = True And ball(6) = True Then
Line11.Visible = True
Player1_WinMsg
ElseIf cross(0) = True And cross(1) = True And cross(2) = True
Then
Line10.Visible = True
Player2_WinMsg
ElseIf cross(3) = True And cross(4) = True And cross(5) = True
Then
Line9.Visible = True
Player2_WinMsg
ElseIf cross(6) = True And cross(7) = True And cross(8) = True
Then
```

```vb
Line8.Visible = True
Player2_WinMsg
ElseIf cross(0) = True And cross(3) = True And cross(6) = True
Then
Line5.Visible = True
Player2_WinMsg
ElseIf cross(1) = True And cross(4) = True And cross(7) = True
Then
Line6.Visible = True
Player2_WinMsg
ElseIf cross(2) = True And cross(5) = True And cross(8) = True
Then
Line7.Visible = True
Player2_WinMsg
ElseIf cross(0) = True And cross(4) = True And cross(8) = True
Then
Line12.Visible = True
Player2_WinMsg
ElseIf cross(2) = True And cross(4) = True And cross(6) = True
Then
Line11.Visible = True
Player2_WinMsg
End If
End Sub


'To check the image has occupied a square or not
Sub check_position()
For m = 0 To 8
If Image1(m).Picture = Image2.Picture Then
ball(m) = True
Else: ball(m) = False
End If


If Image1(m).Picture = Image3.Picture Then
cross(m) = True
Else
cross(m) = False
 End If
 Next
End Sub
```

```vb
Private Sub Image1_Click(Index As Integer)
'To make images (cross or circle) appear on a certain position of
the board
check_position

If player = 1 And cross(Index) = False And ball(Index) = False
Then
Image1(Index).Picture = Image2.Picture
End If
If player = 2 And cross(Index) = False And ball(Index) = False
Then
Image1(Index).Picture = Image3.Picture
End If

check_position
check_status
'To display message for a tie game (if no line visible)
n = n + 1
If n = 9 And Line5.Visible = False And _
Line6.Visible = False And Line7.Visible = False And _
Line8.Visible = False And Line9.Visible = False And _
Line10.Visible = False And Line11.Visible = False And
Line12.Visible = False Then
MsgBox ("Tie!")
newgame
End If

End Sub

Private Sub Image2_Click()
player = 1
End Sub

Private Sub Image3_Click()
player = 2
End Sub

Private Sub mnuNew_Click()
newgame
End Sub
```

```vb
Sub Player1_WinMsg()
MsgBox ("Player1 win!")
newgame2
End Sub


Sub Player2_WinMsg()
MsgBox ("Player2 win!")
newgame2
End Sub


Sub newgame()
n = 0
For m = 0 To 8
Image1(m).Picture = LoadPicture("")
Next
Line5.Visible = False
Line6.Visible = False
Line7.Visible = False
Line8.Visible = False
Line9.Visible = False
Line10.Visible = False
Line11.Visible = False
Line12.Visible = False
End Sub


Sub newgame2()
n = -1
For m = 0 To 8
Image1(m).Picture = LoadPicture("")
Next
Line5.Visible = False
Line6.Visible = False
Line7.Visible = False
Line8.Visible = False
Line9.Visible = False
Line10.Visible = False
Line11.Visible = False
Line12.Visible = False
End Sub
```

The Runtime Interface

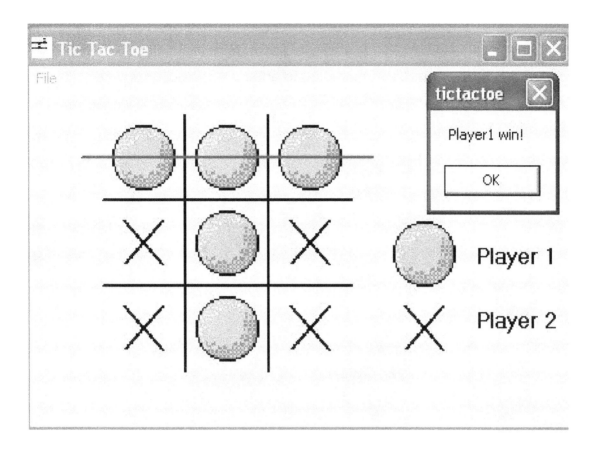

1.12 Time Bomb

This program simulates a time bomb which is ticking away and will explode within 60 seconds. To defuse the bomb, the user need to enter the correct password otherwise the bomb will explode.

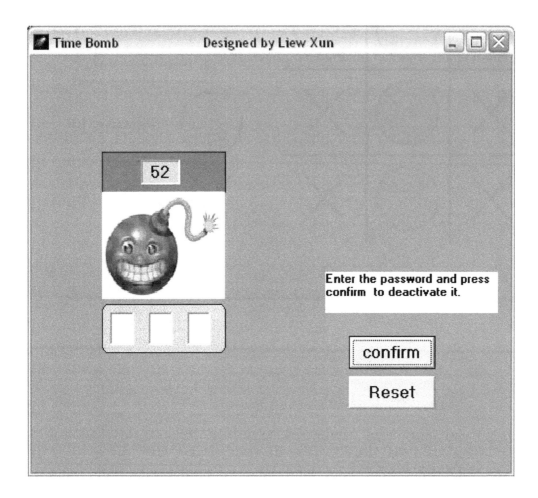

To make the program simpler, the user only needs to key-in a three-digit password which is fixed by the programmer using the declaration. You can also program random password using Rnd function.

```
Const code As Integer = 398
```

To design an attractive interface, you can use the image of a bomb and an image of an exploding bomb. Make the exploding bomb image invisible at startup and make it visible only if the user fails to defuse the bomb. You also need to insert two command buttons, label one of them as **Confirm** and the other one as **Reset**. Besides, insert three text boxes to be used as password panel. Insert a timer control and program it so that it can start the countdown. You can set the timer interval to 1000 so that each countdown is one second or you can set a shorter interval.

You can also insert a **Microsoft Multimedia Control** to play the explosion sound. Note that the Multimedia Control does not appear in the default startup IDE; you need to add it from the component. To do that, go to the menu and click project, select components from the drop-down menu. After choosing **Microsoft Multimedia Control 6.0** from the list of available controls, the multimedia control will appear in the toolbox on the left. To use the Microsoft Multimedia Control, drag the control into the form.

The Code

```
Private Sub Timer1_Timer ()
'To display countdown time, when it is equal to 0, it sets off the
destruction procedure
countdown = 60 - x
If countdown <= 60 And countdown > -1 Then
Lbl_Timer.Caption = Str(countdown)
x = x + 1
ElseIf countdown < 0 Then
Timer1.Enabled = False
destruction
End If
End Sub
 MMControl1.Notify = False
MMControl1.Wait = True
MMControl1.Shareable = False
MMControl1.DeviceType = "WaveAudio"
MMControl1.FileName = "MMControl1.Notify = False"
MMControl1.Wait = True
MMControl1.Shareable = False
MMControl1.DeviceType = "WaveAudio"
MMControl1.FileName = "C:\ My Documents\VB program\audio\bomb.wav"
MMControl1.Command = "Open"
MMControl1.Command = "Play"
```

1.13 Lucky Draw

This is a program that simulates a lucky draw. This program consists of a 3x3 matrix, which means there are nine command buttons in a grid. You need to make the nine command buttons as an array of controls, and you can differentiate them by their indices. One of the buttons contains a prize, when the user clicks on it; it displays the word **"prize"** on the caption. If the user does not strike the prize, the word **"The Prize is here!"** will appear on the command button that contains the prize.

You can use a randomize process and the indices of the command buttons to create the chance events. Random integers from 1 to 9 can be created using the statement **n=Int(Rnd*9)** where **Int** is function that converts numbers to integers and **Rnd** is a method that generates random numbers between 0 and 1.when the user clicks a command button, a random number between 0 and 9 is generated and if this number corresponds to the index of the command button, it will show the word "Prize" on caption of the clicked command button , otherwise, it shows the words "The Prize is here!" on the command button with an index that corresponds to the generated number.

The Interface

The Code

```
Private Sub Command1_Click(Index As Integer)
 Dim n As Integer
      For n = 0 To 8
      Command1(n).Caption = ""
      Next
     n = Int(Rnd * 9)
     If Index = n Then
    Command1(n).Caption = "Prize"
    Else: Command1(n).Caption = "The Prize is here"
    End If
End Sub
```

1.14 Boggle

Boggle is a type of words puzzle game where the players can form as many words as possible from the characters displayed on an nxn square. Words can be formed in many ways, from left to right, from right to left, top to bottom, bottom to top, diagonal, zigzag manner and etc.

The Interface

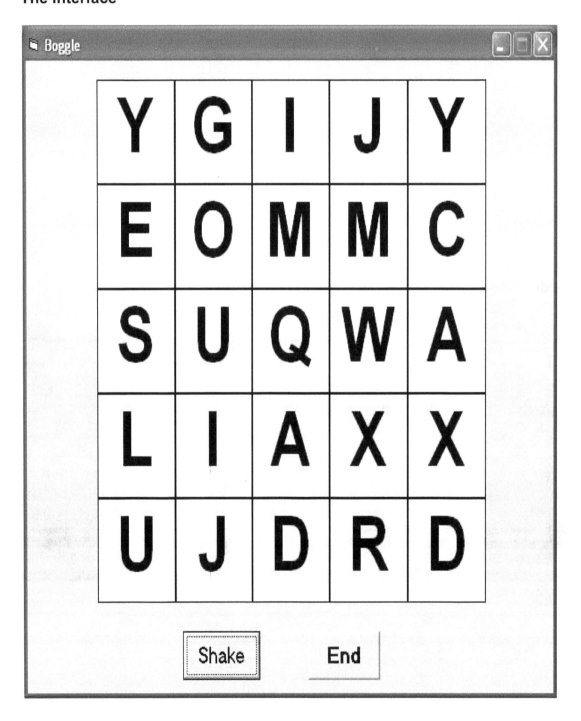

In this program, you can design a 5x5 boggle. Each time a player press the shake button, a different set of characters will appear. In order to do this, you can use the randomize method to generate the characters. In the program, you need to declare an array of 26 characters and displays them on an array of 24 labels by using a For...Next loop.

The Code

```
Dim char(26) As String
Dim I As Integer
Dim J As Integer
Private Sub Command1_Click()
char(0) = "A"
char(1) = "B"
char(2) = "C"
char(3) = "D"
char(4) = "E"
char(5) = "E"
char(6) = "G"
char(7) = "H"
char(8) = "I"
char(9) = "J"
char(10) = "K"
char(11) = "L"
char(12) = "M"
char(13) = "N"
char(14) = "O"
char(15) = "P"
char(16) = "Qu"
char(17) = "R"
char(18) = "S"
char(19) = "T"
char(20) = "U"
char(21) = "V"
char(22) = "W"
char(23) = "X"
char(24) = "Y"
char(25) = "Z"
For I = 0 To 24
```

```
J = Int((Rnd * 26))
Label1(I).Caption = char(J)
Next
End Sub
```

1.15 Hangman Game

The Hangman game is a paper and pencil guessing game for two or more players. The game starts with one player thinks of a word and the other player tries to guess it by suggesting letters within a certain number of guesses.

The hidden word is represented by a row of dashes, representing each letter of the word. If the player correctly guesses a letter in the word, the other player writes it down in all its correct positions. If the suggested letter does not occur in the word, the other player draws one element of a hanged man figure as a tally mark, starting with the head, following by the body then the arm and so forth.

In addition, the guesser has the option of guessing the whole word when he thinks he has enough clues. If the word is correct, the game is over and the guesser wins. Otherwise, the other player penalizes the guesser by adding an element to the diagram. On the other hand, if the guesser commits enough number of incorrect guesses that allows the opponent to complete the hangman diagram, the game is also over, and the guesser loses. However, the guesser can also win by guessing all the letters or numbers that appear in the word, before the diagram is completed.

In our program, we need to draw a hangman diagram. I suggest you use the Line control to draw the diagram. It is also advisable to convert the Line control into a control array so that we can program it easily using a Loop or the If…Then…Else statement. In addition, we also need to place several Label controls onto the form for the purpose of displaying the letters. These Label controls also need to be converted into a control array and also make invisible at startup or replaying the game. Besides that, we also need to place several Line control below the Label control and make them as a control array and invisible at startup. Last but not least, we also need to design a keyboard by placing 26 command buttons onto the form for the user to choose the alphabet. We follow the design of the standard computer keyboard. The buttons must also be converted to a control array.

The Code

```vb
Private Sub CmdKey_Click(Index As Integer)
Dim myletter, myword As String
Dim word(5) As String
Dim hit, count As Integer
hit = Val(Text1.Text) + 1
count = Val(Text2.Text) + 1
Text1.Text = hit
word(0) = "CAT"
word(1) = "DESK"
word(2) = "WATER"
word(3) = "FIRE"
word(4) = "ZEBRA"
word(5) = "EIREE"
myword = alphabet(0).Caption & alphabet(1).Caption &
alphabet(2).Caption & alphabet(3).Caption & alphabet(4).Caption &
alphabet(5).Caption
Select Case Index
Case Is = 0
myletter = "A"
Case Is = 1
myletter = "B"
Case Is = 2
myletter = "C"
Case Is = 3
myletter = "D"
Case Is = 4
myletter = "E"
Case Is = 5
myletter = "F"
Case Is = 6
myletter = "G"
Case Is = 7
myletter = "H"
Case Is = 8
myletter = "I"
Case Is = 9
myletter = "J"
Case Is = 10
myletter = "K"
Case Is = 11
myletter = "L"
Case Is = 12
myletter = "M"
```

```
Case Is = 13
myletter = "N"
Case Is = 14
myletter = "O"
Case Is = 15
myletter = "P"
Case Is = 16
myletter = "Q"
Case Is = 17
myletter = "R"
Case Is = 18
myletter = "S"
Case Is = 19
myletter = "T"
Case Is = 20
myletter = "U"
Case Is = 21
myletter = "V"
Case Is = 22
myletter = "W"
Case Is = 23
myletter = "X"
Case Is = 24
myletter = "Y"
Case Is = 25
myletter = "Z"
End Select
On Error GoTo error_handler
If myletter <> alphabet(0) And myletter <> alphabet(1) And myletter
<> alphabet(2) And myletter <> alphabet(3) And myletter <>
alphabet(4) And myletter <> alphabet(5) Then
count = Val(Text2.Text) + 1
Line1(count).Visible = True
Text2.Text = count
End If




If myletter = alphabet(0) Then
alphabet(0).Visible = True
End If
If myletter = alphabet(1) Then
alphabet(1).Visible = True
```

```
End If
If myletter = alphabet(2) Then
alphabet(2).Visible = True
End If
If myletter = alphabet(3) Then
alphabet(3).Visible = True
End If
If myletter = alphabet(4) Then
alphabet(4).Visible = True
End If
If myletter = alphabet(5) Then
alphabet(5).Visible = True
End If


If count > 4 Then
 MsgBox ("You lost!")
 If myword = word(0) Then
 alphabet(0).Visible = True
 alphabet(1).Visible = True
 alphabet(2).Visible = True
End If
 If myword = word(1) Then
 alphabet(0).Visible = True
 alphabet(1).Visible = True
 alphabet(2).Visible = True
  alphabet(3).Visible = True
 End If
 If myword = word(2) Then
 alphabet(0).Visible = True
 alphabet(1).Visible = True
 alphabet(2).Visible = True
 alphabet(3).Visible = True
 alphabet(4).Visible = True
End If


If myword = word(3) Then
 alphabet(0).Visible = True
 alphabet(1).Visible = True
 alphabet(2).Visible = True
alphabet(3).Visible = True
 End If

  If myword = word(4) Then
```

```vb
 alphabet(0).Visible = True
 alphabet(1).Visible = True
 alphabet(2).Visible = True
 alphabet(3).Visible = True
 alphabet(4).Visible = True
End If
 If myword = word(5) Then
 alphabet(0).Visible = True
 alphabet(1).Visible = True
 alphabet(2).Visible = True
 alphabet(3).Visible = True
 alphabet(4).Visible = True
End If


End If
If count <= 4 Then
If myword = word(0) And alphabet(0).Visible = True And
alphabet(1).Visible = True And alphabet(2).Visible = True Then
MsgBox ("You win!")
End If
If myword = word(1) And alphabet(0).Visible = True And
alphabet(1).Visible = True And alphabet(2).Visible = True And
alphabet(3).Visible = True Then
MsgBox ("You win!")
End If
If myword = word(2) And alphabet(0).Visible = True And
alphabet(1).Visible = True And alphabet(2).Visible = True And
alphabet(3).Visible = True And alphabet(4).Visible = True Then
MsgBox ("You win!")
End If
If myword = word(3) And alphabet(0).Visible = True And
alphabet(1).Visible = True And alphabet(2).Visible = True And
alphabet(3).Visible = True Then

MsgBox ("You win!")
End If
If myword = word(4) And alphabet(0).Visible = True And
alphabet(1).Visible = True And alphabet(2).Visible = True And
alphabet(3).Visible = True And alphabet(4).Visible = True Then
MsgBox ("You win!")
End If
If myword = word(5) And alphabet(0).Visible = True And
```

```vb
alphabet(1).Visible = True And alphabet(2).Visible = True And
alphabet(3).Visible = True And alphabet(4).Visible = True Then
MsgBox ("You win!")
End If
End If
error_handler:
End Sub


Public Sub CmdStart_Click()
generate
End Sub
Sub generate()
Dim num, i As Integer
Dim myChr(), myword As String
Dim word(5) As String
Text1.Text = -1
Text2.Text = -1
For i = 0 To 5
Letter(i).Visible = False
Next
word(0) = "CAT"
word(1) = "DESK"
word(2) = "WATER"
word(3) = "FIRE"
word(4) = "ZEBRA"
word(5) = "EIREE"
For i = 0 To 5
Line1(i).Visible = False
Next
For i = 0 To 5
alphabet(i).Visible = False
alphabet(i).Caption = ""
Next

Randomize Timer
num = Int(Rnd() * 6)
myword = word(num)
If Len(myword) = 3 Then
Letter(0).Visible = True
Letter(1).Visible = True
Letter(2).Visible = True
ElseIf Len(myword) = 4 Then
Letter(0).Visible = True
```

```
Letter(1).Visible = True
Letter(2).Visible = True
Letter(3).Visible = True
ElseIf Len(myword) = 5 Then
Letter(0).Visible = True
Letter(1).Visible = True
Letter(2).Visible = True
Letter(3).Visible = True
Letter(4).Visible = True
End If


For i = 0 To Len(myword) - 1
ReDim myChr(i)
myChr(i) = Mid(myword, i + 1, 1)
alphabet(i) = myChr(i)
Next
End Sub
Public Sub Form_Load()
Dim word(4) As String
Text1.Text = -1
End Sub

Private Sub MenuExit_Click()
Unload Me
End Sub
```

Please refer to the next page for the Interface.

2. Educational Programs

2.1 Kid's Math

This is a simple arithmetic educational game for children. The child who attempts the test can choose three different levels and perform three different arithmetic calculations. The performance can be evaluated by three measurements namely total questions attempted, total correct answers and score which is the percentage of right answers.

The Interface

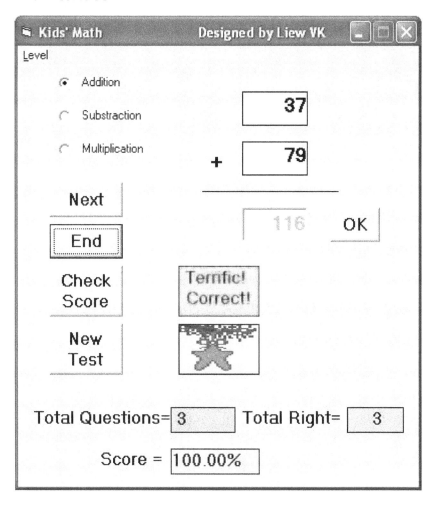

In this program, you need to add the following controls:

- Three option buttons
- Three text boxes
- A few labels
- Two images

The procedure to choose three different arithmetic calculations is

```
Private Sub Option1_Click(Index As Integer)
Select Case Index
Case 0
Label4.Caption = "+"
Action = "Plus"
Case 1
Label4.Caption = "-"
Action = "Minus"
Case 2
Label4.Caption = "x"
Action = "Multiply"
End Select
End Sub
```

The option buttons are grouped together as a control array and can be identified by their indices. Using the Select Case....End Select statements, the caption of Label4 which displays the operators will change according to the selection. In addition, the variable Action will be assigned different values namely "Plus", "Minus" and "Multiply". These values will be passed to the OK procedure and appropriate calculations will be performed.

A menu item "Level" for the user to choose the levels is added using the menu editor. To start the menu editor, you have to click on the tools item on the menu bar. At the menu editor, you key in the word "Level" in the caption box and its name "level" (this can be any appropriate name) in the Name box. This is the first level menu item. To type in the second menu items, you need to click on the Next button and the right arrow key. Here you key in the words Beginner, Intermediate and Advanced. The ampersand sign '&' is used in front of all the captions (it can be in any position) so that the user can use the shortcut key to access the items. For example, to access the Level item, the user can press Alt+L.

You will notice that all the menu items will appear in the code window and you can write the event procedure for each of them. The event procedure for each of the second level menu items is very simple. It simply assigns a value to the variable n, which is n=1 for beginner, n=2 for intermediate and n=3 for advanced.

The procedure to randomize the process of displaying different numbers after each click of the command button "Start" or "Next" (The Start button changes to Next after the first Click) is shown below. The **select Case .....End Select** statements allow the generation of numbers for the three different levels.

```
Select Case n
Case 1
num1 = Int(Rnd * 10)
num2 = Int(Rnd * 10)
Case 2
num1 = Int(Rnd * 90) + 10
num2 = Int(Rnd * 90) + 10
Case 3
num1 = Int(Rnd * 900) + 100
num2 = Int(Rnd * 900) + 100
End Select
```

There are some minor things to be considered before the actual calculation is done. First of all, for subtraction, you need to make sure that the value of the first number is more than the second number as this is arithmetic for kids. This is taken care of using the statement

```
Case "Minus"
If num1 > num2 Then
number1.Caption = num1
number2.Caption = num2
Else
number1.Caption = num2
number2.Caption = num1
End If
```

The above statements ensure that when the second number is larger than the first number, the second number will appear in the first text box and the first number will appear in the second text box. Secondly, to make sure that the multiplication is not too complicated, the second number will be restricted to values between 0 and 10. This can be achieved using the Right function as shown in the following statements:

```
Case "Multiply"
number1.Caption = num1
number2.Caption = Right(num2, 1)
```

The actual calculation is performed under the OK procedure or the KeyPress procedure so that the user has a choice to click the OK button or press the enter key to perform the calculation. The complete code is shown below:

The Code

```
Dim num1 As Integer
Dim num2 As Integer
Dim intNumber As Integer
Dim totalQ As Integer
Dim n As Integer
Dim Action As String
Dim answer As Integer
Dim done As Boolean
Dim score As Integer

Private Sub beginner_Click()
n = 1
End Sub

Private Sub Inter_Click()
n = 2
End Sub

Private Sub advance_Click()
n = 3
End Sub

Private Sub Command3_Click ()
'To calculate the score in percentage
Label10.Caption = Format ((intNumber / totalQ), "Percent")
End Sub

Private Sub Command4_Click()
```

```
total.Caption = ""
Label8.Caption = ""
intNumber = 0
totalQ = 0
Label10.Caption = ""
Command1.Caption = "Start"
End Sub


Private Sub Form_Load()
            n=1
Option1(0).Value = True
Label4.Caption = "+"
Image1.Visible = False
Image2.Visible = False
Label6.Visible = False
Label5.Visible = False
End Sub


Private Sub Option1_Click(Index As Integer)
Select Case Index
Case 0
Label4.Caption = "+"
Action = "Plus"
Case 1
Label4.Caption = "-"
Action = "Minus"
Case 2
Label4.Caption = "x"
Action = "Multiply"
End Select
End Sub


Private Sub Text3_keypress(keyAscii As Integer)
Select Case Action
Case "Plus"
answer = Val(number1.Caption) + Val(number2.Caption)
Case "Minus"
answer = Val(number1.Caption) - Val(number2.Caption)
Case "Multiply"
answer = Val(number1.Caption) * Val(number2.Caption)
End Select
```

```vb
'To response to the pressing of the Enter key
If (keyAscii = 13) And answer = Val(Text3.Text) Then
Image1.Visible = True
Image2.Visible = False
Label5.Visible = True
Label6.Visible = False
If done = True Then
intNumber = intNumber + 1
total.Caption = Str(intNumber)
End If
Text3.Enabled = False
ElseIf (keyAscii = 13) And answer <> Val(Text3.Text) Then
Image1.Visible = False
Image2.Visible = True
Label5.Visible = False
Label6.Visible = True
Text3.Enabled = False
End If
End Sub


Private Sub Command1_Click()
Image1.Visible = False
Image2.Visible = False
Label6.Visible = False
Label5.Visible = False
done = True

Text3.Enabled = True
Text3.Text = ""
x = x + 1
If x > 0 Then
Command1.Caption = "Next"
End If

Randomize Timer
Select Case n
Case 1
num1 = Int(Rnd * 10)
num2 = Int(Rnd * 10)
Case 2
num1 = Int(Rnd * 90) + 10
```

```
num2 = Int(Rnd * 90) + 10
Case 3
num1 = Int(Rnd * 900) + 100
num2 = Int(Rnd * 900) + 100
End Select

Select Case Action
Case "Plus"
number1.Caption = num1
number2.Caption = num2
Case "Minus"
If num1 > num2 Then
number1.Caption = num1
number2.Caption = num2
Else
number1.Caption = num2
number2.Caption = num1
End If
Case "Multiply"
number1.Caption = num1
number2.Caption = Right(num2, 1)
End Select
Text3.SetFocus
totalQ = totalQ + 1
Label8.Caption = Str(totalQ)
End Sub

Private Sub OK_Click()
Select Case Action
Case "Plus"
answer = Val(number1.Caption) + Val(number2.Caption)
Case "Minus"
answer = Val(number1.Caption) - Val(number2.Caption)
Case "Multiply"
answer = Val(number1.Caption) * Val(number2.Caption)
End Select

If Val(Text3.Text) = answer Then
Image1.Visible = True
Image2.Visible = False
Label5.Visible = True
```

```
Label6.Visible = False
If done = True Then
intNumber = intNumber + 1
total.Caption = Str(intNumber)
End If
Else
Image1.Visible = False
Image2.Visible = True
Label5.Visible = False
Label6.Visible = True
End If
Text3.Enabled = False
done = False
End Sub
```

2.2 Pythagorean Theorem

This a program that can solve geometric problems related to Pythagorean Theorem. We supposed everybody is already familiar with the above Theorem. However, some of you may have forgotten the theorem therefore let me explain the theorem here. By referring to a right angled triangle ABC, if the sides are AB, AC and BC respectively, where BC is the hypotenuse, then AB, AC and BC are connected by the formula **AB²+AC²=BC²**

Using the above formula, you can calculate the third sides if the lengths of any two sides are known. For example, if AB=4 and AC=3 then BC=5. You can design the VB program for the user to input any two sides and the program is able to calculate the third side automatically. The third side BC can be found by finding the square root of AB²+AC². In visual basic, the syntax is

```
BC= Sqr(AB ^ 2 + AC ^ 2)
```

You can also use the function **Round** to let the program round the value to two decimal places using the syntax Round (BC, 2).

The Interface

The Code

```
Private Sub Command1_Click()
Dim AB, AC, BC As Single
AB = Val(Txt_AB.Text)
AC = Val(Txt_AC.Text)
BC = Val(Txt_BC.Text)
If AB <> 0 And AC <> 0 Then
BC = Sqr(AB ^ 2 + AC ^ 2)
Txt_BC.Text = Round(BC, 2)
ElseIf AB <> 0 And BC <> 0 Then
AC = Sqr(BC ^ 2 - AB ^ 2)
Txt_AC.Text = Round(AC, 2)
ElseIf AC <> 0 And BC <> 0 Then
AB = Sqr(BC ^ 2 - AC ^ 2)
Txt_AB.Text = Round(AB, 2)
End If
End Sub
```

2.3 Factors Finder

This is a program that can find all the factors of a number entered by the user and displays them in a list box. You can use the simple logic that a number is divisible by all its factors. However, you need to tell Visual Basic how to identify factors from non-factors. In order to do this, you can make use of the fact that the remainder after a number is divided by its factor is zero. In Visual Basic, you can use the **MOD** operator, which compute the value of the remainder after a number is divided by an integer. The format is **N Mod x**.

With these logics in mind, you can use a **For....Next** Loop to evaluate all the remainders for all the divisors of N smaller than N. If the remainder is zero, then the divisor x (factor of x) is added to the list box.

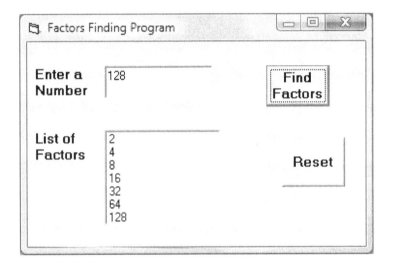

The code

```
Private Sub Command1_Click()
Dim N, x As Integer
N = Val(Text1.Text)
For x = 2 To N - 1
If N Mod x = 0 Then
List1.AddItem (x)
End If
Next
List1.AddItem (N)
End Sub
```

2.4 Prime Number Tester

This program can test whether a number entered by the user is a prime number or not. A prime number is a number that cannot be divided by other numbers other than by itself. Examples are 2, 3, 5, 7, 11, 13, 17, 19, 23, 29, 31, 37 and more.

In this program, you can use the **Select Case ......End Select** statement to determine whether a number entered by a user is a prime number or not. For case 1, all numbers that are less than 2 are not prime numbers. In Case 2, if the number is 2, it is a prime number. In the final case, if the number N is more than 2, you need to divide this number by all the numbers from 3,4,5,6,........up to N-1, if it can be divided by any of these numbers, it is not a prime number, otherwise it is a prime number. To control the program flow, you can use the **Do......Loop While** statement. Besides, you need to use **tag="Not Prime'** to identify the number that is not prime, so that when the routine exits the loop, the label will display the correct answer.

The Interface

The Code

```
Private Sub Command1_Click()
Dim N, D  As  Single
Dim tag As String


N = Val(TxtNumber.Text)


Select Case N
Case Is < 2
Lbl_Answer.Caption = "It is not a prime number"
Case Is = 2
Lbl_Answer.Caption = "It is a prime number"
Case Is > 2
D = 2
Do
If N / D = Int(N / D) Then
Lbl_Answer.Caption = "It is not a prime number"
tag = "Not Prime"
Exit Do
End If
D = D + 1
Loop While D <= N - 1
If tag <> "Not Prime" Then
Lbl_Answer.Caption = "It is a prime number"
End If
End Select
End Sub
```

2.5 Geometric Progression

This is a program that generates a geometric progression and displays the results in a list box. Geometric progression is a sequence of numbers where each subsequent number is found by multiplying the previous number by a fixed number which is called common ratio. The common ratio can be negative, an integer, a fraction and any number but it must not be a zero. The I formula to find the nth term of the geometric progression is

$$ar^{n-1}$$

Where a is the first number and r is the common ratio.

In visual basic, you can employ the **Do.... Loop Until** statement to generate the numbers in a geometric progression. In this program, you need to insert three text boxes for the user to enter the first number, the common ratio and the number of terms. You also need to insert a list box to list the numbers. Besides that, a command button is need for the user to generate the numbers in the geometric progression. To add the numbers to the list box, you can use the **AddItem** method. The syntax is **List1.AddItem** n, where n can be any variable.

The Code

```
Private Sub cmd_compute_Click()
Dim x, n, num As Integer
Dim r As Single
x = Txt_FirstNum.Text
r = Txt_CR
num = Txt_Terms.Text
List1.AddItem "n" & vbTab & "x"
List1.AddItem "_____"

n = 1
Do
x = x * r
List1.AddItem n & vbTab & x
n = n + 1
Loop Until n = num + 1
End Sub
```

The Interface

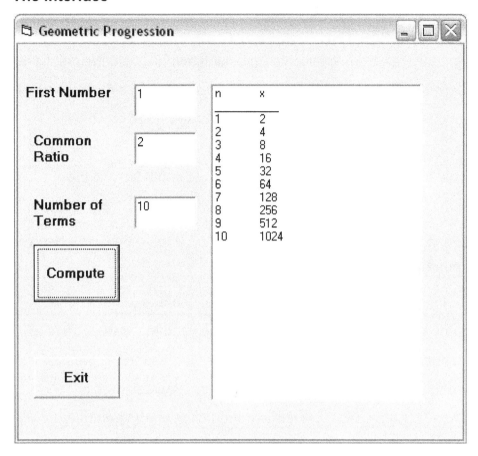

2.6 Maximum Number Calculator

This program allows the user enters three hidden numbers and it can calculate the maximum number among the three numbers. In order for the user type the password in a hidden mode, you have to set the PasswordChar property to alphanumeric symbols such as *.

Now, you can create a function called **calMax** that consists of three arguments **x, y, z** .You also need to write a procedure to call this function. This procedure employs the **If Then ElseIf** statements and the conditional operators to determine the maximum number. The function **Str** is used to convert a numeric to string.

The Code

```
Function calMax(x, y, z As Variant)
If x > y And x > z Then
calMax = Str(x)
ElseIf y > x And y > z Then
calMax = Str(y)
ElseIf z > x And z > y Then
calMax = Str(z)
End If
End Function


Private Sub Command1_Click()
Dim a, b, c
a = Val(Txt_Num1.Text)
b = Val(Txt_Num2.Text)
c = Val(Txt_Num3.Text)
Lbl_Display.Caption = calMax(a, b, c)
End Sub
```

The Interface

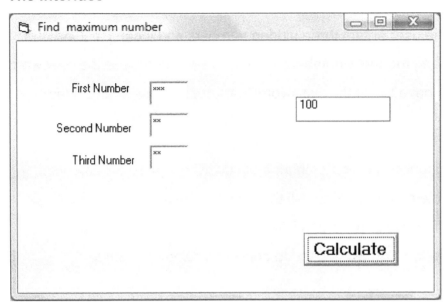

2.7 Quadratic Equation Solver

Quadratic equation is a fairly straight forward high school mathematics problem. The quadratic equation solver was programmed to determine the number of roots the equation has as well as to compute the roots. It uses the determinant b^2 -4ac to solve the problems. If b^2 -4ac>0, then it has two roots and if b^2 -4ac=0, then it has one root, else it has no root. To obtain the roots, the program uses the standard quadratic formula as follows:

$$X = -b \pm \sqrt{\frac{b^2 - 4ac}{2a}}$$

The Code

```
Private Sub Form_Load()
Dim a, b, c, det As Integer
Dim root1, root2 As Single
Dim numroot As Integer
End Sub


Private Sub new_Click()
' To set all values to zero
Coeff_a.Text = ""
Coeff_b.Text = ""
Coeff_c.Text = ""
Answers.Caption = ""
txt_root1.Visible = False
txt_root2.Visible = False
txt_root1.Text = ""
txt_root2.Text = ""
Lbl_and.Visible = False
Lbl_numroot.Caption = ""
End Sub
```

```
Private Sub Solve_Click()
a = Val(Coeff_a.Text)
b = Val(Coeff_b.Text)
c = Val(Coeff_c.Text)

'To compute the value of the determinant
det = (b ^ 2) - (4 * a * c)
If det > 0 Then
Lbl_numroot.Caption = 2
root1 = (-b + Sqr(det)) / (2 * a)
root2 = (-b - Sqr(det)) / (2 * a)
Answers.Caption = "The roots are "
Lbl_and.Visible = True
txt_root1.Visible = True
txt_root2.Visible = True
txt_root1.Text = Round(root1, 4)
txt_root2.Text = Round(root2, 4)
ElseIf det = 0 Then
root1 = (-b) / 2 * a
Lbl_numroot.Caption = 1
Answers.Caption = "The root is "
txt_root1.Visible = True
txt_root1.Text = root1
Else
Lbl_numroot.Caption = 0
Answers.Caption = "There is no root "
End If
End Sub
```

The Interface

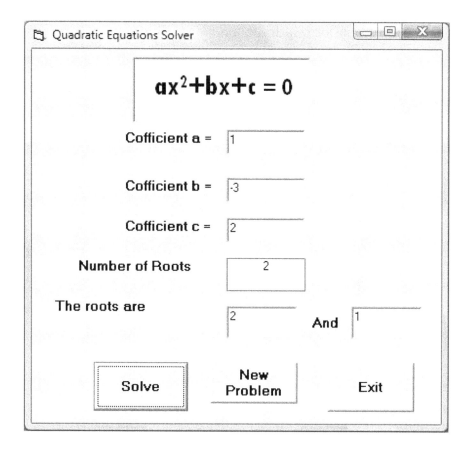

2.8 Quadratic Functions Graph Plotter

This is a program that can plot graphs for quadratic functions. The general format of a quadratic equation is $f(x) = ax^2+bx+c$, where a, b and c are constant. This program is a useful tool for high school teachers to teach mathematics. This program employs a picture box as the plot area and three text boxes to obtain the values of the coefficients a, b, c of the quadratic equation from the user. You need to modify the scale factor in the properties windows of the picture box. You can use a scale of 0.5 cm to represent 1 unit.

Besides, you need to make some transformation as the coordinates in VB start from top left but you want it to start from the middle. You can use the **Pset** method to draw the graph using a very small increment. Pset is a method that draws a dot on the screen, the syntax is

Pset(x, y), color

Where (x, y) is the coordinates of the dot and colour is the colour of the dot. The default color is black. Using the For Next loop together with Pset, the program can draw a line on the screen.

The Code

```
Private Sub cmd_draw_Click()
Dim a, b, c As Integer
Dim w, v As Single
a = Val(txt_a.Text)
b = Val(txt_b.Text)
c = Val(txt_c.Text)
'Using a scale of 0.5 cm to represent i unit to draw the graph
For w = 0 To 10 Step 0.001
v = a * (5 - w) ^ 2 - b * (5 - w) + c
pic_graph.PSet (w, 5 - v)
Next w
End Sub

Private Sub Command1_Click()
```

```
pic_graph.Cls
txt_a.Text = ""
txt_b.Text = ""
txt_c.Text = ""
End Sub
```

The Interface

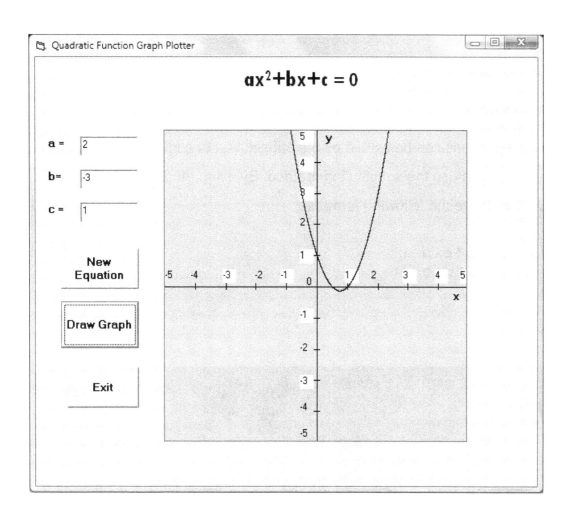

2.9 Simultaneous Equations Solvers

2.9(a) Linear Simultaneous Equations

Simultaneous equations are equations that involve two or more unknown variables. There must be as many equations as the number of unknown variables in order for us to solve the problem. In this example, we shall only solve linear simultaneous equations. Linear simultaneous equations take the following forms:

$$ax+by= m$$

$$cx+by = n$$

Simultaneous equations can be solved by the substitution or elimination methods. In this program, you can use the substitution method. By using the aforementioned method you can derive the following formulas:

$$x = (b * n - d * m) / (b * c - a * d)$$
$$y = (a * n - c * m) / (a * d - b * c)$$

The Code

```vb
Private Sub Solve_Click()
Dim a, b, c, d, m, n As Integer
Dim x, y As Double

a = Val(Txt_a.Text)
b = Val(Txt_b.Text)
m = Val(Txt_m.Text)
c = Val(Txt_c.Text)
d = Val(Txt_d.Text)
n = Val(Txt_n.Text)
x = (b * n - d * m) / (b * c - a * d)
y = (a * n - c * m) / (a * d - b * c)
Lbl_x.Caption = Round(x, 2)
Lbl_y.Caption = Round(y, 2)    'using round to limit decimal places

End Sub
```

```
    'To get new equations

Private Sub New_Click()
Txt_a.Text = ""
Txt_b.Text = ""
Txt_m.Text = ""
Txt_c.Text = ""
Txt_d.Text = ""
Txt_n.Text = ""
Lbl_x.Caption = ""
Lbl_y.Caption = ""

End Sub
```

The Interface

2.9(b) Mixed Simultaneous Equations

In this example, we will show you how to design a program that can solve mixed simultaneous equations, that is, one linear equation and one quadratic equation. Mixed simultaneous equations take the following forms:

$$ax+by=m$$

$$cx^2+dy^2=n$$

Simultaneous equations can normally be solved by the substitution or elimination methods. In this program, you can use the substitution method. So, you can obtain the following formulas:

$$x_1 = (m\,a\,d + Sqr(m^2\,a^2\,d^2 - (b^2\,c + a^2\,d)\,(d\,m^2 - b^2\,n)))\,/\,(b^2\,c + a^2\,d)$$
$$x_2 = (m\,a\,d +\text{-}Sqr(m^2\,a^2\,d^2 - (b^2\,c + a^2\,d)\,(d\,m^2 - b^2\,n)))\,/\,(b^2\,c + a^2\,d)$$

$$y_1 = (m - a\,x_1)\,/\,b$$
$$y_2 = (m - a\,x_2)\,/\,b$$

The Code

```
Private Sub Command1_Click()
Dim a, b, c, d, m, n As Integer
Dim x1, x2, y1, y2 As Double

a = Val(Txt_a.Text)
b = Val(Txt_b.Text)
m = Val(Txt_m.Text)
c = Val(Txt_c.Text)
d = Val(Txt_d.Text)
n = Val(Txt_n.Text)
x1 = (m * a * d + Sqr(m ^ 2 * a ^ 2 * d ^ 2 - (b ^ 2 * c + a ^ 2 *
d) * _
(d * m ^ 2 - b ^ 2 * n))) / (b ^ 2 * c + a ^ 2 * d)

x2 = (m * a * d - Sqr(m ^ 2 * a ^ 2 * d ^ 2 - (b ^ 2 * c + a ^ 2 *
d) *_
```

```
  (d * m ^ 2 - b ^ 2 * n))) / (b ^ 2 * c + a ^ 2 * d)
y1 = (m - a * x1) / b
y2 = (m - a * x2) / b
Lbl_x1.Caption = Round(x1, 2)
Lbl_y1.Caption = Round(y1, 2)
Lbl_x2.Caption = Round(x2, 2)
Lbl_y2.Caption = Round(y2, 2)

End Sub
```

The Interface

2.10. The Sine Rule

The Sine Rule can be used to calculate the remaining sides of a triangle when two angles and a side are known. It can also be used when two sides and one of the non-enclosed angles are known. In some cases, the formula may produce two possible values for the enclosed angle, leading to an ambiguous case. The sine rule is shown below.

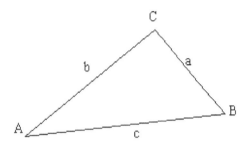

By referring to the figure above, the formula of the sine rule is:

$$\frac{a}{\sin A} = \frac{b}{\sin B} = \frac{c}{\sin C} = D$$

For example, if the user enters angle A and angle B as 60 and 30 respectively, and the length a=4, then b=6.93. You need to convert the degree to radian by multiplying the angle by π(=3.14159) and divide it by 180.

The Code

```
Private Sub Cal_Click()
Dim A, B, l, X, Y, d As Single
Const Pi as Single=3.14159
A = Val(Txt_angleA.Text)
B = Val(Txt_angleB.Text)
l = Val(Txt_sideA.Text)
'To convert the angle to radian
X = (Pi / 180) * A
Y = (Pi / 180) * B
```

```
b = l * Sin(X) / Sin(Y)
'To correct the answer to two decimal places
Lbl_Answer.Caption = Str(Format(b, "0.00"))
End Sub
```

The Interface

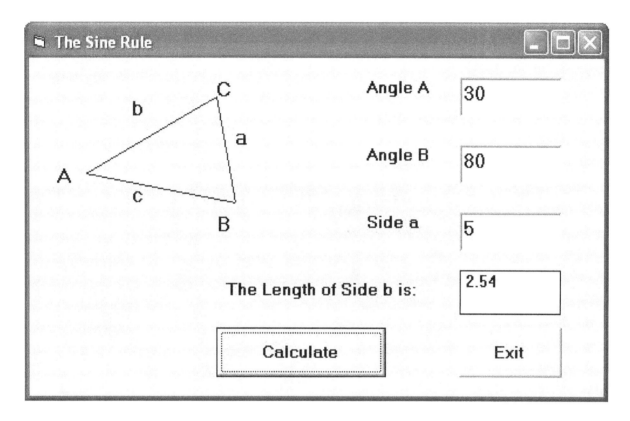

2.11 Projectile

This is a program that can plot the path of a projectile, a basic concept of missile launching. This path is determined by the launching angle and speed. The formula is $y=(V\sin a)\,t-\frac{1}{2}(gt^2)$ and $x=(V\cos a)t$, where **V=launching speed** and **a** is the launching angle, **g** is acceleration due to gravity(9.8 ms^{-2}) while **t** is the flight time.

In this program, you can use a picture box for drawing the parabolic curve. The command Pset is used to plot the curve. Pset is a method that draws a point on the screen. Using a looping procedure like the Do ..... Loop will connect all the points into a line.

The Code

```
Private Sub cmd_Draw_Click()
Dim x, y, v, t, a As Single
v = Txt_Speed.Text
a = Txt_Angle.Text
Pic_Curve.Cls

Do
t = t + 0.01
y = v * Sin(a * 3.141592654 / 180) * t - 4.9 * (t ^ 2)
x = v * Cos(a * 3.141592654 / 180) * t
Pic_Curve.PSet (x, 120 - y)
If x > 120 Then
Exit Do
End If
Loop
End Sub
```

The Interface

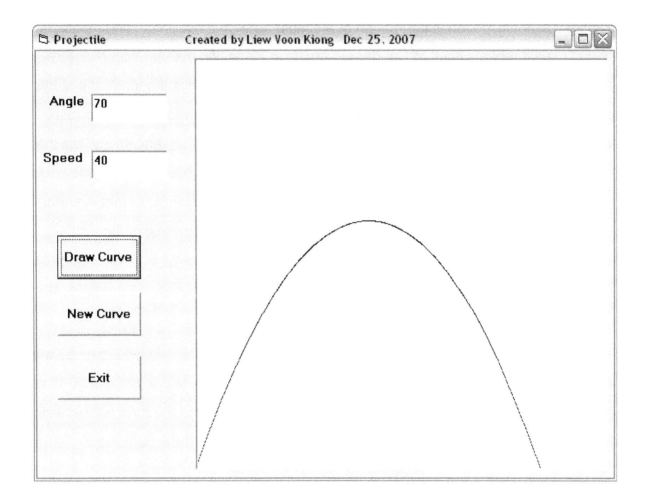

2.12 Simple Harmonic Motion

Simple harmonic motion is the motion of a simple harmonic oscillator. The motion is periodic, as it repeats itself at standard intervals in a specific manner with constant amplitude. It is characterized by its amplitude, its period which is the time for a single oscillation, its frequency which is the number of cycles per unit time, and its phase, which determines the starting point on the sine wave. The period, and its inverse the frequency, are constants determined by the overall system, while the amplitude and phase are determined by the initial conditions (position and velocity) of that system. (Wikipedia, 2008). The general equation describing simple harmonic motion is

x=Acos(2pft+f), where x is the displacement, A is the amplitude of oscillation, f is the frequency, t is the elapsed time, and f is the phase of oscillation.

To create a simple model of simple harmonic motion in Visual Basic, you can use the equation **x=Acos(wt),** and you can assign a value of 500 to A and a value of 50 to w. In this program, the circular object which has been inserted into the form will oscillate from left to right, reaching the maximum speed at the middle of the path.

In this program, you have to insert a shape and set it to be a circle in the properties windows. Next, insert two command buttons and change the captions to start and stop respectively. Finally, insert a timer and set its interval to be 100 and disabled it at startup. You can use the move method to move the shape1 object whose path is determined by the formula **x = 500 * Cos (50 * t).** When you run the program, the object will move in an oscillating motion as shown in the figure below:

The Code

```
Dim t As Integer

Private Sub cmd_Start_Click()

Timer1.Enabled = True

End Sub
```

```
Private Sub cmd_Stop_Click()

Timer1.Enabled = False
End Sub

Private Sub Timer1_Timer()

t = t + 1
x = 500 * Cos(50 * t)
Shape1.Move Shape1.Left + x

End Sub
```

The Interface

3. Financial Programs

3.1 Amortization Calculator

Before we delve into the program code, you need to know some basic financial concepts. The term loan amortization means the computation of the amount of equal periodic payments necessary to provide lender with a specific interest return and repay the loan principal over a specified period. The loan amortization process involves finding the future payments whose present value at the loan interest rate equal the amount of initial principal borrowed. Lenders use a loan amortization schedule to determine these payment amounts and the allocation of each payment to interest and principal.

The formula to calculate periodic payment is

$$\text{Payment} = \frac{Initial\ Principal}{PVIFA}$$

PVIFA is known as present value interest factor for an annuity. The formula to compute PVIFA is

$$PVIFA = \frac{1}{i} - \frac{1}{i(1+i)^n}$$

Where n is the number of payments. Normally you can check up a financial table for the value of PVIFA and then calculate the payments manually. You can also use a financial calculator to compute the values. However, if you already know how to write program in VB, why not create your very own financial calculator.

To calculate the payments for interest, you can multiply the initial principal with the interest rate, and then use periodic payment to minus payment for interest. To calculate the balance at the end of a period, you can use the formula

End-of-year principal=Beginning-of-year principal - periodic payment

In this program, you need to add four text boxes to accept the input for initial principal value, number of payments, interest rate per annum and amount of periodic payments. You also need to insert a list box to display the amortization table.

The Code

```
Dim Num, n As Integer
Dim I, P, PVIFA, r, pmt, PI, PP As Double

Public Sub Cmd_Calculate_Click()

P = Txt_Principal.Text
Num = Txt_Num_payment.Text
r = Txt_Interest.Text
I = r / 100
PVIFA = 1 / I - 1 / (I * (1 + I) ^ Num)
pmt = P / PVIFA
Lbl_Amtpayment.Caption = Round(pmt, 2)

End Sub

Private Sub Cmd_Create_Click()

List_Amortization.AddItem "n" & vbTab & "Periodic" & vbTab & vbTab
& "Payment" & vbTab & vbTab & "Payment" & vbTab & vbTab &
"Balance"
List_Amortization.AddItem "" & vbTab & "Payment" & vbTab & vbTab &
"Interest" & vbTab & vbTab & "Principal"
List_Amortization.AddItem
"_____     "
Do
n = n + 1
PI = P * I
PP = pmt - PI
P = P - PP
List_Amortization.AddItem n & vbTab & Round(pmt, 2) & vbTab &
vbTab & Round(PI, 2) & vbTab & vbTab & Round(PP, 2) & vbTab &
vbTab & Round(P, 2)
If n = Num Then
```

```
Exit Do
End If


Loop


End Sub
```

The Interface

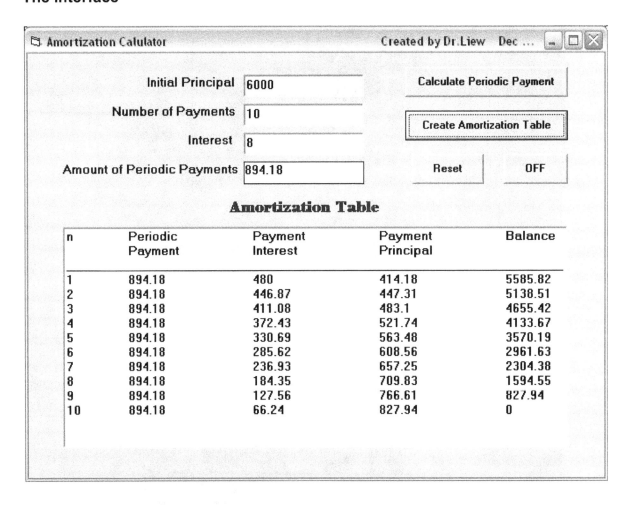

3.2 Depreciation Calculator

Depreciation means a reduction in the value of an asset with the passage of time. Depreciation is computed based on the initial purchase price or initial cost, number of years where depreciation is calculated, salvage value at the end of the depreciation period, and the asset's life span.

Depreciation is an important element in the management of a company's assets. With proper and accurate calculation of depreciation, a company can benefit from the tax advantage. In Visual Basic, The syntax of the depreciation function is

DDB(Cost,Salvage,Life, Period)

Cost=Initial cost, Salvage=Salvage value, Life=Asset's life span

Period=Depreciation period

In this program, you need to add four text boxes to accept input for initial cost, salvage value, asset's life and period of depreciation. Besides that, insert a label to display the amount of depreciation and a command button to compute the depreciation.

The Code

```
Private Sub Command1_Click()

Dim Int_Cost, Sal_Value, Asset_Life, Deperiod, Depre_Amt As Double
Int_Cost = Val(Txt_Cost.Text)
Sal_Value = Val(Txt_Salvage.Text)
Asset_Life = Val(Txt_Life.Text)
Deperiod = Val(Txt_Period.Text)
Depre_Amt = DDB(Int_Cost, Sal_Value, Asset_Life, Deperiod)
Lbl_Dpre.Caption = Format(Depre_Amt, "$###,###,000.00")

End Sub
```

The Interface

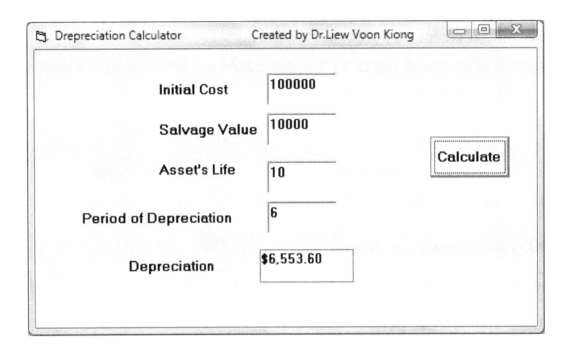

3.3 Future Value Calculator

The concept of future value is related to time value of money. For example, if you deposit your money in a bank as a savings account or a fixed deposit account for a certain period of time, you will earn a certain amount of money based on the compound interest computed periodically, and this amount is added to the principal if you continue to keep the money in the bank. Interest for the following period is now computed based on the initial principal plus the interest (the amount which becomes your new principal). Subsequent interests are computed in the same way.

For example, let's say you deposited $1000 in a bank and the bank is paying you 5% compound interest annually. After the first year, you will earn an interest of $1000x0.05=$50.

Your new principal will be

$1000+$1000x0.05=$1000(1+0.05)=$1000(1.05)=$1050.

After the second year, your new principal will be

$1000(1.05)x1.05=$1000(1.05)2 =$1102.50.

This new principal is called the future value.

Following the above calculation, the future value after n years will be

$$FV = PV *(1+ \frac{i}{100})^n$$

Where PV represents the present value, FV represents the future value , i is the interest rate and n is the number of periods (Normally months or years).

The code

```
Public Function FV(PV As Variant, i As Variant, n As Variant) As
Variant
'Formula to calculate Future Value(FV)
'PV denotes Present Value
FV = PV * (1 + i / 100) ^ n
End Function
```

```
Private Sub compute_Click()
'This procedure calculates the Future Value
Dim FutureVal As Currency
Dim PresentVal As Currency
Dim interest As Variant
Dim period As Variant
PresentVal = PV.Text
interest = rate.Text
period = years.Text
FutureVal = FV(PresentVal, interest, period)
Label5.Caption = Format(FutureVal, "currency")
End Sub
```

The Interface

3.4 Investments Calculator

This program is basically the same as the Future Value Calculator in the previous section, where you can use the formula

$$FV = PV * \left(1 + \frac{i}{100} \right)^n$$

to calculate the future value. However, in this example, we assume you have a target future value in mind and you wish to know how much money you need to invest to achieve the target based on a certain interest. Though you still can employ the same basic formula, this time you can use the Visual Basic 6 built-in present value function, or PV.

The syntax of the PV function is

PV(Rate,Nper, Pmt,FV,Due)

Rate=Interest rate

Nper=The length of period (Usually number of years)

Pmt=Periodic payment

 FV=Future Value

*Due= 1 if payment due at beginning of a period and Due=0 if payment due at the end of a period. In our example, you can consider a single initial investment in order to earn a certain amount of money in the future, so Pmt is set to 0, and payment due is at the beginning of the period, so it is set at 0, the rest of the values are obtained from the users.

The Code

```
Private Sub cmdCal_Click()
Dim F_Money, Int_Rate, Investment As Double
Dim numYear As Single
F_Money = Val(Txt_FV.Text)
Int_Rate = (Val(Txt_Rate.Text) / 100)
```

```
numYear = Val(Txt_Year.Text)
Investment = PV(Int_Rate, numYear, 0, F_Money, 1)
Lbl_PV.Caption = Format(-Investment, "$##,###,##0.00")
End Sub
```

The Interface

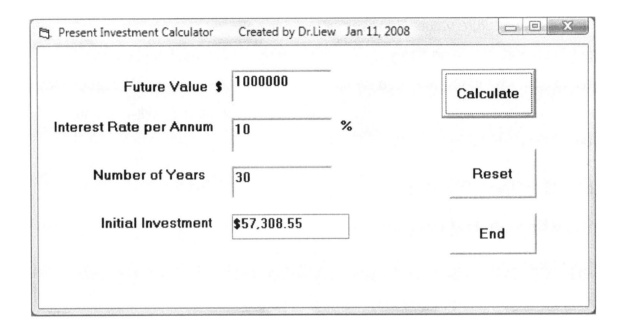

3.5 Payback Period Calculator

Currently people seem to face a lot of difficulties to secure a loan or have problem to pay back a loan. The subprime loan issues seem to hit everyone hard. Still, we need to borrow money every now and then to acquire an asset or to pay for education fees. So, naturally we need to find out how long we can settle a loan for a certain amount of monthly payment at a certain interest rate. It is not easy to calculate such figure; fortunately Visual Basic comes to the rescue. There is built-in function in VB to calculate the payback period is Nper and the syntax is

Nper(Rate,Pmt,PV,FV,Due)

Rate=Interest Rate

Pmt=Amount of Periodic Payment

PV=Loan taken

FV=Future Value (set to 0 if loan is settled)

Due=set to 1 if payment at the beginning of the period

     set to 0 if payment at the end of the period

The Code

```
Private Sub Command1_Click()
Dim payment, Loan, Int_Rate As Double
Dim Num_year As Single
payment = Val(Txt_Payment.Text)
Int_Rate = (Val(Txt_Rate.Text) / 100) / 12
Loan = Val(Txt_PV.Text)
Num_year = NPer(Int_Rate, payment, -Loan, 0, 0) / 12
Lbl_Period.Caption = Str(Int(Num_year))

End Sub
```

The Interface

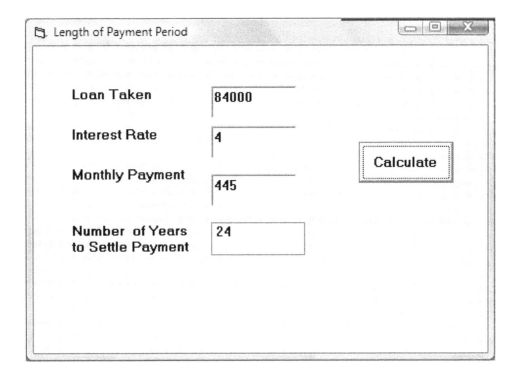

3.6 Stock Trading Simulation Program

We can create a stock trading simulation program easily using Visual Basic 6. Of course, you can also create the program using other versions of Visual Basic.

For stock trading, we need to consider the following data:

- Asking Price- Price offered by the sellers
- Bidding Price- Price offered by the buyers
- Selling Quantity-Total number of shares available for sale on the stock market
- Buying Quantity- Total number of shares the buyers bid on the stock market
- Last Done Price- The price for the last transaction
- Order Price – Price bid by the trader to buy or to sell
- Order Quantity- Number of Shares ordered by the trader
- Average Price- Average share price
- Buy Value – Average value of shares paid by the trader
- Gross Market Value- The current market of shares owned by the trader
- The total number of shares in the hand of the trader.
- Profit or Loss

We shall use the following variables to represent the aforementioned data:

AP- Asking Price

BD- Bidding Price

SQ- Selling Quantity

BQ- Buying Quantity

LP- Last Done Price

OP- Order Price

OQ- Order Quantity

AVP- Average Price

BV- Buy Value

MV- Gross Market Value

TQ- Total Number of Shares in Hand

In this program, we need to insert a timer to generate random values for the Asking Price, the Bidding Price, the Selling Quantity, the Buying Quantity and the Last Done Price. You can set the timer to any interval you think is suitable, here we set it to 15 seconds so that the values changes every 15 seconds to simulate the real stock market. The code is as follows:

ranNum1 = Rnd() * 2 + 3

ranNum2 = Rnd() * 2 + 3

ranNum3 = Rnd() * 2 + 3

AP = Round(ranNum1, 3) * 5

SQ = Int (Round(Rnd (), 2) * 10000) + 1000

BD = Round(ranNum2, 3) * 5

BQ = Int(Round(Rnd(), 2) * 10000) + 1000

LP = Round(ranNum3, 3) * 5 'Last Done Price

LVOL = Int(Round(Rnd(), 2) * 10000) + 1000 'Last Done Volume

PL- Profit or Loss

Besides that, we need to write code to calculate the Average Price, the Buy Value, the Gross Market Value and the total number of shares in hand, as follows:

$$AVP = (AVP * TQ + OP * OQ) / (TQ + OQ)$$

$$TQ = TQ + OQ$$

$$MV = LP * TQ$$

$$BV = TQ * AVP$$

The Code

```
Dim ranNum1, ranNum2, randNum3, ranNum4 As Double
Dim AP As Single
Dim SQ As Integer
Dim BD As Single
Dim BQ As Integer
Dim OQ As Long
Dim OP As Single
Dim LP As Single
Dim LVOL As Integer
Dim AVP As Single
Dim TQ As Long
Dim BV As Single
Dim MV As Single
Dim PL As Single


Private Sub Cmd_Submit_Click()
OQ = Val(Txt_Quantity.Text)
OP = Val(Txt_Price.Text)
LP = Lbl_LP.Caption
If Opt_Buy.Value = True And BV >= 1000 Then
AVP = (AVP * TQ + OP * OQ) / (TQ + OQ)
TQ = TQ + OQ
Lbl_TQ.Caption = TQ
MV = LP * TQ
BV = TQ * AVP
PL = MV - BV
Lbl_LP.Caption = Format(LP, "#,##.00")
Lbl_MV.Caption = Format(MV, "#,##.00")
Lbl_BV.Caption = Format(BV, "#,##.00")
```

```vb
Lbl_PL.Caption = Format(PL, "#,##.00")
Lbl_PL.Caption = Format(PL, "#,##.00")
Lbl_AVP.Caption = Format(AVP, "#,##.00")
ElseIf Opt_Buy.Value = True And BV < 1000 Then
MsgBox ("You don't have enough fund to buy, reduce order")
End If


If Opt_Sell.Value = True And TQ >= OQ Then
AVP = (AVP * TQ + OP * OQ) / (TQ + OQ)
TQ = TQ - OQ
Lbl_TQ.Caption = TQ
MV = LP * TQ
BV = TQ * AVP
PL = MV - BV
Lbl_MV.Caption = Format(MV, "#,##.00")
Lbl_BV.Caption = Format(BV, "#,##.00")
Lbl_PL.Caption = Format(PL, "#,##.00")
Lbl_AVP.Caption = Format(AVP, "#,##.00")


ElseIf Opt_Sell.Value = True And TQ < OQ Then
MsgBox ("Not enough shares, reduce order")
End If
End Sub


Private Sub Form_Load()
Randomize
ranNum1 = Rnd() * 2 + 3
ranNum2 = Rnd() * 2 + 3
ranNum3 = Rnd() * 2 + 3
ranNum4 = Rnd() * 2 + 3
AVP = Round(ranNum1, 3) * 5 ' Average Price
TQ = Int(Round(Rnd(), 2) * 10000) + 1000 'Total Shares at Hand
BV = AVP * TQ 'Buy Value
AP = Round(ranNum2, 3) * 5 'Asking Price
SQ = Int(Round(Rnd(), 2) * 10000) + 1000
BD = Round(ranNum2, 3) * 5 'Bidding Price
BQ = Int(Round(Rnd(), 2) * 10000) + 1000
LP = Round(ranNum2, 3) * 5 'Last Done Price
MV = LP * TQ
PL = MV - BV
LVOL = Int(Round(Rnd(), 2) * 10000) + 1000 'Last Done Volume
```

```vb
Lbl_AP.Caption = AP
Lbl_SQ.Caption = SQ
Lbl_BD.Caption = BD
Lbl_BQ.Caption = BQ
Lbl_LP.Caption = OP
Lbl_AVP.Caption = AVP
Lbl_TQ.Caption = TQ
Lbl_MV.Caption = Format(MV, "#,##.00")
Lbl_PL.Caption = Format(PL, "#,##.00")
Lbl_LP.Caption = Format(LP, "#,##.00")
Lbl_BV.Caption = Format(BV, "#,##.00")
Lbl_Vol.Caption = LVOL
End Sub


Private Sub Timer1_Timer()
Randomize
ranNum1 = Rnd() * 2 + 3
ranNum2 = Rnd() * 2 + 3
ranNum3 = Rnd() * 2 + 3
AP = Round(ranNum1, 3) * 5
SQ = Int(Round(Rnd(), 2) * 10000) + 1000
BD = Round(ranNum2, 3) * 5
BQ = Int(Round(Rnd(), 2) * 10000) + 1000
LP = Round(ranNum3, 3) * 5 'Last Done Price
MV = LP * TQ ' Market Value
PL = MV - BV
LVOL = Int(Round(Rnd(), 2) * 10000) + 1000 'Last Done Volume
Lbl_AP.Caption = AP
Lbl_SQ.Caption = SQ
Lbl_BD.Caption = BD
Lbl_BQ.Caption = BQ
Lbl_LP.Caption = LP
Lbl_Vol.Caption = LVOL
Lbl_MV.Caption = Format(MV, "#,##.00")
Lbl_PL.Caption = Format(PL, "#,##.00")
End Sub
```

The Design Interface

The Runtime Interface

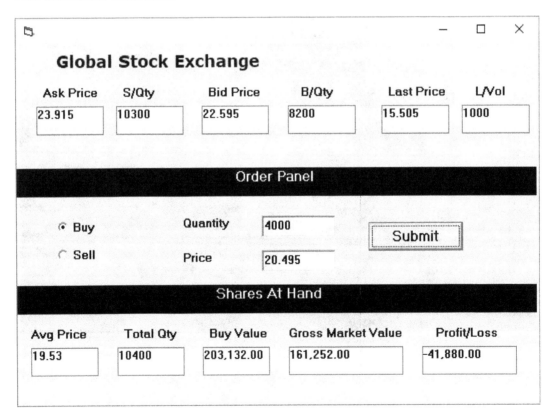

4. Graphics Programs

4.1 Drawing Pad

You can create a simple virtual drawing program using Visual Basic 6. You may call it drawing pad.

In this program, the user needs to fill in all the coordinates and chooses a colour before he or she can proceed to draw the required shape. If he or she forgets to fill in the coordinates or chooses a colour, he or she will be prompted to do so.

To create the drawing pad, you need to insert a common dialog control, a picture box, four text boxes, six command buttons and the necessary labels. The function of the common dialog control is to assist the users to choose colours. The text boxes are for the user to enter the coordinates and the picture box is to display the pictures drawn.

The syntax to draw a straight line is Line, and the syntax is as follows:

```
Picture1.Line (x1, y1)-(x2, y2), color
```

Where picture1 is the picture box, (x1, y1) is the coordinates of the starting point, (x2, y2) is the ending point and color understandably is the color of the line.

The syntax to draw a non-solid rectangle is

```
Picture1.Line (x1, y1)-(x2, y2), color, B
```

The syntax to draw a solid rectangle is

```
Picture1.Line (x1, y1)-(x2, y2), color, BF
```

The syntax to draw a circle is

```
Picture1.Circle (x3, y3), r, color
```

(x 3, y3) the center of the circle, and r is the radius.

If you wish to draw a solid circle and fill it with the selected color, then add two more lines to the above syntax:

```
Picture1.FillStyle = vbSolid
Picture1.FillColor = color
```

The syntax to clear the picture is

```
Picture1.Cls
```

The code

```
Private Sub cmd_Rectangle_Click()
x1 = Text1.Text
y1 = Text2.Text
x2 = Text3.Text
y2 = Text4.Text
Picture1.Line (x1, y1)-(x2, y2), color, B
End Sub

Private Sub cmd_Color_Click()
CommonDialog1.Flags = &H1&
CommonDialog1.ShowColor
color = CommonDialog1.color
End Sub

Private Sub cmd_Circle_Click()

On Error GoTo addvalues
x3 = Text5.Text
y3 = Text6.Text
r = Text7.Text
Picture1.FillStyle = vbSolid
Picture1.FillColor = color
Picture1.Circle (x3, y3), r, color
```

```
Exit Sub
addvalues:
MsgBox ("Please fill in the coordinates ,the radius and the
color")
End Sub


Private Sub Command5_Click()
Picture1.Cls
End Sub


Private Sub cmd_SolidRect_Click()
x1 = Text1.Text
y1 = Text2.Text
x2 = Text3.Text
y2 = Text4.Text
Picture1.Line (x1, y1)-(x2, y2), color, BF
End Sub
```

The Interface

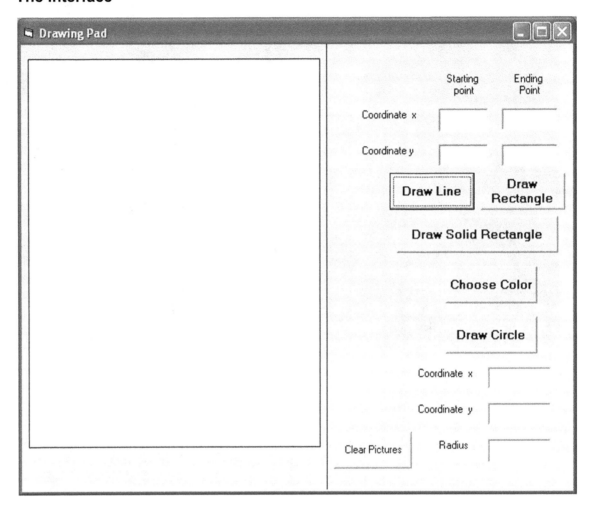

4.2 Picture Viewer

This is a program that enables the user browse, open and chooses image files from the folders in his or her computer and views them in a picture box. There are two ways to implement the program. The first is to build the program from the ground up and the second makes use of the common dialog box.

The first way is a little more complicated but you can learn a great deal of programming techniques. To create this program, you need to insert a drive list box(**DriveListBox**) , a directory list box (**DirListBox**), a file list box(**FileListBox**) and a combo box . The drive list box is for the user to select a drive, the directory list box is for the user to choose a folder and the file list box is display the files in the selected folder. Besides that, the combo box allows the user to select all graphics files or all files. You also need to insert a picture box to display the image.

The code for First Method

```
Private Sub Combo1_Change()
'To list all graphics files or all files
If ListIndex = 0 Then
File1.Pattern = ("*.bmp;*.wmf;*.jpg;*.gif")
Else
Fiel1.Pattern = ("*.*")
End If
End Sub
Private Sub Dir1_Change() 'To choose drive
File1.Path = Dir1.Path
File1.Pattern = ("*.bmp;*.wmf;*.jpg;*.gif")
End Sub

Private Sub Drive1_Change()
Dir1.Path = Drive1.Drive
End Sub

Private Sub File1_Click()
'To select a file
If Combo1.ListIndex = 0 Then
```

```
File1.Pattern = ("*.bmp;*.wmf;*.jpg;*.gif")
Else
File1.Pattern = ("*.*")
End If

If Right(File1.Path, 1) <> "\" Then
filenam = File1.Path + "\" + File1.FileName
Else
filenam = File1.Path + File1.FileName
End If
End Sub

Private Sub show_Click()
'To show the selected graphics file
If Right(File1.Path, 1) <> "\" Then
filenam = File1.Path + "\" + File1.FileName
Else
filenam = File1.Path + File1.FileName
End If
Picture1.Picture = LoadPicture(filenam)
End Sub
```

The Code for Second Method

The second way is much easier to program, you only need to insert an image control, a common dialog box and an icon that resembles on opened file. You need to set the stretchable property of the image control to true. The procedure to open the common dialog box to browse the image files as well as to load the selected picture into the image control is

```
CommonDialog1.Filter =
"Bitmaps(*.BMP)|*.BMP|Metafiles(*.WMF)|*.WMF|Jpeg
Files(*.jpg)|*.jpg|GIF Files(*.gif)|*.gif|Icon
Files(*.ico)|*.ico|All Files(*.*)|*.*"
CommonDialog1.ShowOpen
Picture1.Picture = LoadPicture(CommonDialog1.FileName)
```

The filter property of the common dialog box uses the format as shown below

Bitmaps(*.BMP)|*.BMP

To specify the file type, and uses the pipe line | to separate different file types. Visual Basic supports most of the picture formats namely bmp, wmf, jpg, gif, ico(icon) and cur(cursor) files.

The command **CommonDialog1.ShowOpen** is to open the common dialog box and the command

```
Picture1.Picture = LoadPicture (CommonDialog1.FileName)
```

is to load the selected picture file into the picture box.

The whole program is shown below and the output is shown in the figure below:

```
Private Sub Image1_Click()
CommonDialog1.Filter =
"Bitmaps(*.BMP)|*.BMP|Metafiles(*.WMF)|*.WMF|Jpeg
Files(*.jpg)|*.jpg|GIF Files(*.gif)|*.gif|Icon
Files(*.ico)|*.ico|All Files(*.*)|*.*"
CommonDialog1.ShowOpen
image2.Picture = LoadPicture (CommonDialog1.FileName)
End Sub
```

The second way is much easier to program, you only need to insert an image control, a common dialog box and an icon that resembles on opened file. You need to set the stretchable property of the image control to true. The procedure to open the common dialog box to browse the image files as well as to load the selected picture into the image control is

```
CommonDialog1.Filter =
"Bitmaps(*.BMP)|*.BMP|Metafiles(*.WMF)|*.WMF|Jpeg
Files(*.jpg)|*.jpg|GIF Files(*.gif)|*.gif|Icon
Files(*.ico)|*.ico|All Files(*.*)|*.*"
```

```
CommonDialog1.ShowOpen
Picture1.Picture = LoadPicture(CommonDialog1.FileName)
```

The filter property of the common dialog box uses the format as shown below

Bitmaps(*.BMP)|*.BMP

to specify the file type, and uses the pipe line | to separate different file types. Visual Basic supports most of the picture formats namely bmp, wmf, jpg, gif, ico(icon) and cur(cursor) files. The command *CommonDialog1.ShowOpen* is to open the common dialog box and the command

```
Picture1.Picture = LoadPicture (CommonDialog1.FileName)
```

is to load the selected picture file into the picture box.

The Code

```
Private Sub Image1_Click()
CommonDialog1.Filter =
"Bitmaps(*.BMP)|*.BMP|Metafiles(*.WMF)|*.WMF|Jpeg _
Files(*.jpg)|*.jpg|GIF Files(*.gif)|*.gif|Icon
Files(*.ico)|*.ico|All _ Files(*.*)|*.*"
CommonDialog1.ShowOpen
image2.Picture = LoadPicture (CommonDialog1.FileName)
End Sub
```

When the user clicks the opened file icon, the following dialog will appear. The user then can select the file he or she wishes to view.

The Interface

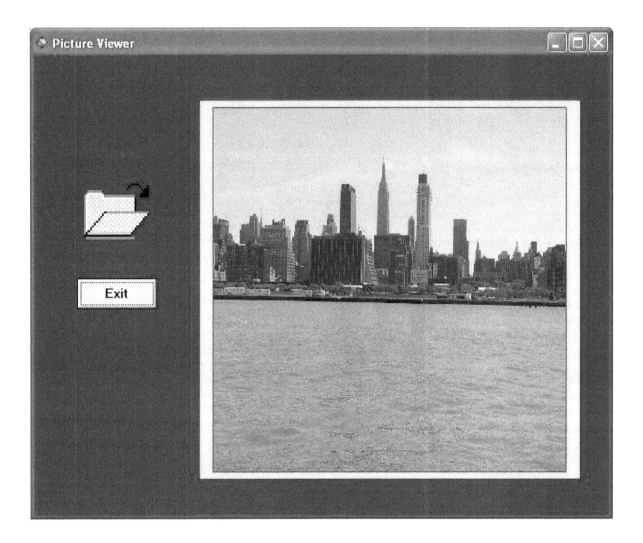

5 Multimedia Programs

In Visual Basic, you can create various multimedia applications that can play audio CD, DVD, various audio files including mp3, wav and midi files; and different types of video files such as avi, mpeg files and etc. To be able to play multimedia files or multimedia devices, you have to insert the **Microsoft Multimedia Control** into your applications that you are going to create. However, Microsoft Multimedia Control is not normally included in the startup toolbox. Therefore, you need to add the Microsoft Multimedia control by pressing Ctrl+T and checking the box beside the **Microsoft Multimedia control 6.0** from the components that are displayed in the dialog box as shown in the figure below and then press the OK button. When you close the dialog box, you will notice that the Microsoft Multimedia Control will be available in the toolbox and you can drag it into the form.

5.1 Creating a DVD Player

In this program, you will insert the Microsoft Multimedia Control and set its properties to Visible:True as well as Play: Enabled. In addition, insert five command buttons and name as well as label them as **Play, Next, Previous, Stop** and **Exit**. Besides that, insert a label that can be used to display the current track number of the song being played. Lastly, enter the program codes.

The most important statement in this program is to set the Microsoft Multimedia Control's device type to CDAudio because it will ensure an audio CD or DVD can be played.

```
MMControl1.DeviceType = "CDAudio"
```

To display the track number of the current song being played, use the following statement:

```
trackNum.Caption = MMControl1.Track
```

The Play, Next, Previous and Stop commands can be programmed using the following statements

```
MMControl1.Command = "Play"
MMControl1.Command = "Next"
MMControl1.Command = "Prev"
MMControl1.Command = "Stop"
```

Lastly, always ensure that the Microsoft Multimedia Control is closed whenever the user closes the player. This can be achieved by using the statement under the **Form1_Unload** procedure.

```
MMControl1.Command = "Close"
```

The Code

```
Private Sub Form_Load ()
'To position the page at the center of the screen
Left = (Screen.Width - Width) \ 2
Top = (Screen.Height - Height) \ 2
End Sub


Private Sub Form_Activate ()
'Load the CDPlayer
MMControl1.Notify = False
MMControl1.Wait = True
MMControl1.DeviceType = "CDAudio"
MMControl1.Command = "Open"
End Sub


Private Sub MMControl1_StatusUpdate ()
'Update the track number
trackNum.Caption = MMControl1.Track
End Sub


Private Sub Next_Click ()
MMControl1.Command = "Next"
End Sub


Private Sub Play_Click ()
MMControl1.Command = "Play"
End Sub


Private Sub Previous_Click ()
MMControl1.Command = "Prev"
End Sub


Private Sub Stop_Click ()
MMControl1.Command = "Stop"
End Sub


Private Sub Exit_Click ()
MMControl1.Command = "Stop"
MMControl1.Command = "Close"
```

```
Unload Me
End Sub
Private Sub Form1_unload ()
'Unload the CDPlayer
MMControl1.Command = "Close"
End Sub
```

The DVD Player Interface

5.2 A Smart Audio Player

In the preceding section, you have programmed a DVD player. Now, with some minor modifications, you will transform the DVD player into an audio player. This player will be created in such a way that it can search for wav and midi files in your drives and play them. In this project, you need to insert a ComboBox, a DriveListBox, a DirListBox, a TextBox and a FileListBox into your form. I shall briefly discuss the function of each of the above controls. Besides that, you must also insert Microsoft Multimedia Control (MMControl) in your form. You may make it visible or invisible. In this program, I choose to make it invisible so that I can use the command buttons created to control the player. The functions of the various controls are explained below:

a) The ComboBox

Displays and enables the selection of different types of files. To add items to the Combo Box, you can use the AddItem method. The items here are the extensions of different audio files.

b) The DriveListBox

The DriveListBox allows the selection of different drives in your computer.

c) The DirListBox

The DirListBox displays different directories that are available in your computer.

d) The Textbox

The Textbox displays the selected files.

e) The FileListBox

The FileListBox displays files that are available in your computer.

Relevant codes must be written to coordinate all the above controls so that the application can work properly. The program should flow in the following logical steps:

Step 1: User chooses the type of files he wants to play.

Step2: User selects the drive that might contain the relevant audio files.

Step 3: User looks into directories and subdirectories for the files specified in step 1. The files should be displayed in the FileListBox.

Step 4: User selects the files from the FileListBox and clicks the Play button.

Step 5: User clicks on the Stop button to stop playing and the Exit button to end the application.

To coordinate the DriveListBox and the DirListBox, you can use the statement below, so that any change of the drives will be reflected in the directory list box.

```
Dir1.Path = Drive1.Drive
```

To coordinate the FileListBox and the DirListBox, you can use the statement below so that any change of the directories will be reflected in the File List Box.

```
File1.Path = Dir1.Path
```

To select the target file, you can use the following statements where File1.Path determines the path of the file and File1.FileName determines the file name. The file name is then assigned to the variable filename and displayed in the textbox.

```
If Right (File1.Path, 1) <> "\" Then
filenam = File1.Path + "\" + File1.FileName
Else
filenam = File1.Path + File1.FileName
End If
Text1.Text = filenam
```

To select the file types, you can use the statement File1.Pattern = ("*.wav") to choose the wave audio files and the statement File1.Pattern = ("*.mid") to choose the sequencer files.

To play the selected file, use the following procedure:

```
Private Sub play_Click ()
'To play WaveAudio file or Midi File
If Combo1.ListIndex = 0 Then
MMControl1.DeviceType = "WaveAudio"
ElseIf Combo1.ListIndex = 1 Then
MMControl1.DeviceType = "Sequencer"
End If
```

```
MMControl1.FileName = Text1.Text
MMControl1.Command = "Open"
MMControl1.Command = "Play"
End Sub
```

The statement

```
MMControl1.DeviceType = "WaveAudio"
```

enables the Microsoft Multimedia Control to play Wav Audio files.

The statement

```
MMControl1.DeviceType = "Sequencer"
```

enables the Microsoft Multimedia Control to play the midi files. In fact, the Microsoft Multimedia Control can play many other types of multimedia files, including Mpeg, Mp3 and Avi video files.

The statement

```
MMControl1.FileName = Text1.Text
```

plays the multimedia file displayed in the Text1 textbox.

The statement

```
MMControl1.Command = "Open"
```

initiates the Microsoft Multimedia Control.

The statement

```
MMControl1.Command = "Play"
```

plays the multimedia file.

The statement

```
MMControl1.Command = "stop"
```

stops the Microsoft Multimedia Control from playing.

The statement

```
MMControl1.Command = "Close"
```

closes the Microsoft Multimedia Control.

The Code

```
Private Sub Form_Load ()
'To center the Audioplayer
Left = (Screen.Width - Width) \ 2
Top = (Screen.Height - Height) \ 2
Combo1.Text = "*.wav"
Combo1.AddItem "*.wav"
Combo1.AddItem "*.mid"
Combo1.AddItem "All files"
End Sub

Private Sub Combo1_Change ()
'To determine file type
If ListIndex = 0 Then
File1.Pattern = ("*.wav")
ElseIf ListIndex = 1 Then
File1.Pattern = ("*.mid")
Else
Fiel1.Pattern = ("*.*")
End If
End Sub

Private Sub Dir1_Change ()
'To change directories and subdirectories (or folders and
subfolders)
```

```
File1.Path = Dir1.Path
If Combo1.ListIndex = 0 Then
File1.Pattern = ("*.wav")
ElseIf Combo1.ListIndex = 1 Then
File1.Pattern = ("*.mid")
Else
File1.Pattern = ("*.*")
End If
End Sub


Private Sub Drive1_Change ()
'To change drives
Dir1.Path = Drive1.Drive
End Sub


Private Sub File1_Click ()
If Combo1.ListIndex = 0 Then
File1.Pattern = ("*.wav")
ElseIf Combo1.ListIndex = 1 Then
File1.Pattern = ("*.mid")
Else
File1.Pattern = ("*.*")
End If
If Right(File1.Path, 1) <> "\" Then
filenam = File1.Path + "\" + File1.FileName
Else
filenam = File1.Path + File1.FileName
End If
Text1.Text = filename
End Sub


Private Sub play_Click ()
'To play WaveAudio file or Midi file
If Combo1.ListIndex = 0 Then
MMControl1.DeviceType = "WaveAudio"
ElseIf Combo1.ListIndex = 1 Then
MMControl1.DeviceType = "Sequencer"
End If
MMControl1.FileName = Text1.Text
MMControl1.Command = "Open"
MMControl1.Command = "Play"
```

```
End Sub

Private Sub stop_Click ()
MMControl1.Command = "Stop"
End Sub

Private Sub Exit_Click ()
MMControl1.Command = "Close"
Unload Me
End Sub

Private Sub Drive1.Change()
Dir1.Path=Drive1.Drive
End Sub
```

Smart Audio Player Interface

5.3 Multimedia Player

In the preceding section, you have created an audio player. Now, by making some minor modifications, you will transform the audio player into a multimedia player that can play all kinds of movie files besides audio files. This player will be created in such a way that it can search for all types of media files in your computer drives and play them.

In this project, you need to insert a ComboBox, a DriveListBox, a DirListBox, a TextBox, a FileListBox, and a picture box (for playing movies) into your form. I shall briefly discuss the function of each of the above controls. You must also insert Microsoft Multimedia Control (MMControl) in your form; you may make it visible or invisible. In my program, I choose to make it invisible so that I can use the command buttons created to control the player.

The program is almost similar to the audio player, but you need to add a few extra statements so that you can play the video files and also the mp3 files. First of all, you have to add two more file types with the statements

```
File1.Pattern = ("*.avi")
```

and

```
File1.Pattern = ("*.mpeg;*.mpg;*.mp3")
```

so that the Avi and Mpeg movie files as well as the mp3 files will show up in the file list box . Secondly, you have to add the statement

```
MMControl1.DeviceType = " "
```

so that the Microsoft Multimedia Control can play the Avi video files and the statement

```
MMControl1.DeviceType = " "
```

so that the player can play other media files such as the mp3 files.

The Code

```
Private Sub Form_Load ()
Left = (Screen.Width - Width) \ 2
Top = (Screen.Height - Height) \ 2
Combo1.Text = "*.wav"
Combo1.AddItem "*.wav"
Combo1.AddItem "*.mid"
Combo1.AddItem "*.avi"
Combo1.AddItem "*.mpeg;*.mpg;*.mp3"
Combo1.AddItem "All files"
End Sub


Private Sub Combo1_Change ()
If ListIndex = 0 Then
File1.Pattern = ("*.wav")
ElseIf ListIndex = 1 Then
File1.Pattern = ("*.mid")
ElseIf ListIndex = 2 Then
File1.Pattern = ("*.avi")
ElseIf ListIndex = 3 Then
File1.Pattern = ("*.mpeg;*.mpg;*.mp3")
Else
Fiel1.Pattern = ("*.*")
End If
End Sub


Private Sub Dir1_Change ()
File1.Path = Dir1.Path
If Combo1.ListIndex = 0 Then
File1.Pattern = ("*.wav")
ElseIf Combo1.ListIndex = 1 Then
File1.Pattern = ("*.mid")
ElseIf Combo1.ListIndex = 2 Then
File1.Pattern = ("*.avi")
ElseIf Combo1.ListIndex = 3 Then
File1.Pattern = ("*.mpeg;*.mpg;*.mp3")
Else
File1.Pattern = ("*.*")
End If
End Sub
```

```
Private Sub Drive1_Change ()
Dir1.Path = Drive1.Drive
End Sub


Private Sub File1_Click ()
If Combo1.ListIndex = 0 Then
File1.Pattern = ("*.wav")
ElseIf Combo1.ListIndex = 1 Then
File1.Pattern = ("*.mid")
ElseIf Combo1.ListIndex = 2 Then
File1.Pattern = ("*.avi")
ElseIf Combo1.ListIndex = 3 Then
File1.Pattern = ("*.mpeg;*.mpg;*.mp3")
Else
File1.Pattern = ("*.*")
End If
If Right (File1.Path, 1) <> "\" Then
filenam = File1.Path + "\" + File1.FileName
Else
filenam = File1.Path + File1.FileName
End If
Text1.Text = filename
End Sub


Private Sub Exit_Click ()
MMControl1.Command = "Close"
Uload Me
End Sub


Private Sub Open_Click ()
If Combo1.ListIndex = 0 Then
MMControl1.DeviceType = "WaveAudio"
End If
If Combo1.ListIndex = 1 Then
MMControl1.DeviceType = "Sequencer"
End If
If Combo1.ListIndex = 2 Then
MMControl1.DeviceType = "AVIVideo"
End If
If Combo1.ListIndex = 3 Then
```

```
MMControl1.DeviceType = ""
End If
MMControl1.FileName = Text1.Text
MMControl1.Command = "Open"
End Sub


Private Sub play_Click ()
Timer1.Enabled = True
MMControl1.Command = "Play"
MMControl1.hWndDisplay = Picture1.hWnd
End Sub


Private Sub stop_Click ()
If MMControl1.Mode = 524 Then
Exit Sub
If MMControl1.Mode <> 525 Then
MMControl1.Wait = True
MMControl1.Command = "Stop"
End If
MMControl1.Wait = True
MMControl1.Command = "Close"
End Sub
```

The Interface

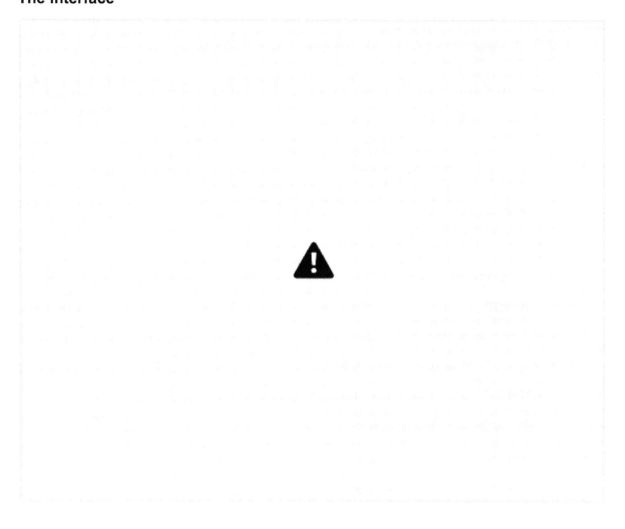

5.4 Windows Media Player

This is a VB6 Windows media player that can play all kinds of media files such as wav, midi, mp3, mpeg video, avi video and more. When you launch the program, you can select media files of different types from different sources such as your hard drives, CD and even the URL of a webpage . After you have selected a particular file, you can play it using the customized button or you can use the buttons of the Windows Media Player

In this program, you need to insert the Windows Media Player Control. This control is not available in the default VB6 IDE, you have to press CTRl+T keys to bring up the components dialog, and check the Windows Media Player then click OK, as shown in Figure 1. In addition, you need to insert Microsoft Common Dialog Control 6.0 into the form. This control is also not available in the default IDE, press CTRL+T to bring up the components windows and check on this control, as shown in the Figure 2.

Figure 1

Figure 2

Now you are ready to design the player's interface. First, drag the Windows Media Player control into the form and reside it to a certain size. Set its fullScreen property to false. Next, insert Microsoft Common Dialog Control 6.0 in the form and then insert five command buttons in the form. Change the caption of first button to Open, second one to Play, third one to Close, fourth one to Exit and the last one to Full Screen. Finally, insert a text box for the purpose to display the URL of the selected media file. The design would look like the one shown in Figure 3.

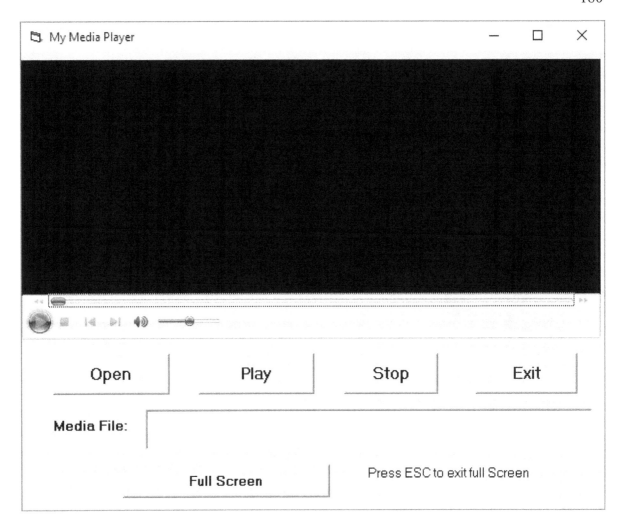

Figure 3

6 Tools and Utilities

6.1 BMI Calculator

Many people are obese nowadays so much so it is affecting their health seriously. If a person's BMI is more than 30, he or she is considered obese. You can refer to the following range of BMI values for the weight status.

- Underweight = <18.5
- Normal weight = 18.5-24.9
- Overweight = 25-29.9
- Obesity = BMI of 30 or greater
-

This BMI calculator is a Visual Basic program that can calculate the body mass index, or BMI of a person based on the body weight in kilogram and the body height in meter. BMI can be calculated using the formula

$$\frac{weight}{height^2}$$

*weight is measured in kg and height in meter. If you only know your weight and height in lb. and feet, then you need to convert them to the metric system.

The Code

```
Private Sub Command1_Click ()
Label4.Caption = BMI (Text1.Text, Text2.Text)
End Sub

Private Function BMI (height, weight)
BMIValue = (weight) / (height ^ 2)
BMI = Format (BMIValue, "0.00")
End Function
```

The Interface

6.2 Calculator

This is a typical calculator that consists of the number buttons, the operator buttons and some additional buttons such as the memory button and the clear button.

To design the interface, you need to insert 25 command buttons, and one label that functions as the display panel. The number buttons from 1 to 9 are grouped together as a control array and named as ButtonNum while 0 is a standalone command and named as Bzero. The four basic operators are also grouped together as a control array and named as Operator. Other buttons are named appropriately according to their functions. The label is named as panel.

One of the most important procedures in the program is to control the display on the panel. The procedure is

```
Private Sub ButtonNum_Click(Index As Integer)
If Num_of_digit > 0 Then
If Num_of_digit < 30 Then
panel. Caption = panel.Caption + Right$(Str(Index), 1)
Num_of_digit = Num_of_digit + 1
End If
Else
panel.Caption = Right$(Str(Index), 1)
Num_of_digit = 1
End If
CheckValue
End Sub
```

The Num_of_digit is a variable that is used to check the number of digits that appear on the display panel. The procedure will ensure that if the number of digits is more than one, the preceding digit will be pushed to the left and the succeeding digit will remain on the right. However, if the number of digits is zero, the digit clicked will just appear on the rightmost position of the panel.

Another important procedure is the procedure to perform the calculations. This can be achieved through the Operator and the Equal sub procedures. The Operator sub procedure is shown below:

```
Private Sub Operator_Click(Index As Integer)
CheckValue
If Index = 11 Then
a = displayValue
key = 1
ElseIf Index = 12 Then
b = displayValue
key = 2
ElseIf Index = 13 Then
c = displayValue
key = 3
ElseIf Index = 14 Then
d = displayValue
key = 4
ElseIf Index = 15 Then
f = displayValue
key = 5
End If
Num_of_digit = 0
newNumber = True
End Sub
```

This procedure ensures that when a particular operator button is pressed, the variable key is assigned a number so that the program knows which operator is being pressed. The calculation is then executed using the Equal sub procedure which is shown below:

```
Private Sub Equal_Click()
CheckValue
If newNumber = True Then
If key = 1 Then
e = displayValue + a
ElseIf key = 2 Then
```

```
e = b - displayValue
ElseIf key = 3 Then
e = displayValue * c
ElseIf key = 5 Then
e = (f * displayValue) / 100
ElseIf key = 4 And displayValue <> 0 Then
e = d / displayValue
Else
GoTo error
End If
If Abs(e) < 1 Then
panel.Caption = Format(e, "General Number")
Else
panel.Caption = Str(e)
End If
Else
panel.Caption = displayValue
End If
GoTo finish
error: panel.Caption = "E"
finish:
Num_of_digit = 0
newNumber = False

End Sub
```

The displayValue is the value that is displayed on the panel and this value is checked through the CheckValue sub procedure. The statements

```
If Abs(e) < 1 Then
panel.Caption = Format(e, "General Number")
Else
panel.Caption = Str(e)
End If
```

are to ensure that when the absolute value is less than 0, the zero appears in front of the decimal point, for example, 0.5 instead of just .5. The whole program is shown below:

The Code

```vb
Option Explicit
Dim Num_of_digit As Integer
Dim key As Integer
Dim displayValue As Variant
Dim a, b, c, d, e, f, g As Variant
Dim memo As Variant
Dim newNumber As Boolean


Private Sub BZero_Click(Index As Integer)
If Num_of_digit > 0 Then
panel.Caption = panel.Caption + "0"
Else
panel.Caption = "0"
Num_of_digit = Num_of_digit + 1
End If
CheckValue
End Sub


Sub CheckValue()
displayValue = Val(panel.Caption)
End Sub


Private Sub ButtonNum_Click(Index As Integer)
If Num_of_digit > 0 Then
If Num_of_digit < 30 Then
panel.Caption = panel.Caption + Right$(Str(Index), 1)
Num_of_digit = Num_of_digit + 1
End If
Else
panel.Caption = Right$(Str(Index), 1)
Num_of_digit = 1
End If
CheckValue
End Sub
```

```
Private Sub Clear_Click()
panel.Caption = "0"
displayValue = "0"
Num_of_digit = 0
End Sub


Private Sub ClearAll_Click()
panel.Caption = "0"
displayValue = "0"
memo = 0
End Sub


Private Sub Equal_Click()

CheckValue
If newNumber = True Then
If key = 1 Then
e = displayValue + a
ElseIf key = 2 Then
e = b - displayValue
ElseIf key = 3 Then
e = displayValue * c
ElseIf key = 5 Then
e = (f * displayValue) / 100
ElseIf key = 4 And displayValue <> 0 Then
e = d / displayValue
Else
GoTo error
End If
If Abs(e) < 1 Then
panel.Caption = Format(e, "General Number")
Else
panel.Caption = Str(e)
End If
Else
panel.Caption = displayValue
End If
GoTo finish
error: panel.Caption = "E"
finish:
Num_of_digit = 0
```

```vb
newNumber = False
End Sub


Private Sub MemoCancel_Click()
memo = 0
End Sub


Private Sub Memory_Click()
CheckValue
memo = displayValue
Num_of_digit = 0
End Sub


Private Sub Operator_Click(Index As Integer)
CheckValue
If Index = 11 Then
a = displayValue
key = 1
ElseIf Index = 12 Then
b = displayValue
key = 2
ElseIf Index = 13 Then
c = displayValue
key = 3
ElseIf Index = 14 Then
d = displayValue
key = 4
ElseIf Index = 15 Then
f = displayValue
key = 5
End If
Num_of_digit = 0
newNumber = True

End Sub


Private Sub Plus_minus_Click()
CheckValue
g = -1 * displayValue
displayValue = g
panel.Caption = Str(displayValue)
```

```
CheckValue
End Sub


Private Sub Poin_Click()
Static point_lock As Integer
If point_lock = 0 And Num_of_digit < 20 Then
panel.Caption = panel.Caption + "."
Num_of_digit = Num_of_digit + 1
End If
CheckValue
End Sub


Private Sub Recall_Click()
panel.Caption = Str(memo)
End Sub


Private Sub SqRoot_Click()
CheckValue
If displayValue >= 0 Then
panel.Caption = Str(Sqr(displayValue))
Else
panel.Caption = "E"
End If
Num_of_digit = 0
End Sub


Private Sub Summation_Click()
CheckValue
memo = memo + displayValue
Num_of_digit = 0
End Sub
```

The Interface

6.3 Digital Clock

Visual Basic programming is so simple that sometime you just need to write a one line code to create a wonderful tiny little but nice application. For example, you can write a one-line code to create a digital clock.

In this program, you have to insert a timer control into the form. Then go to the properties window to set the timer interval value to 1000 so that Visual Basic updates the time every 1000 milliseconds, or once a second. Other properties that you ought to set are to change the caption such as "My Clock" and to set Form1 MaxButton to false so that it cannot be resized by the user.

Now, double click the timer and enter the one line code as follows:

```
Private Sub Timer1_Timer()
  Label1.Caption = Time
End Sub
```

The Design Interface

The Output Interface

6.4 Polling System

Survey and polling tools are often used in marketing or politics to assess ratings for certain services or products. Polling tools can take many forms, some just use a simple dichotomous scale of Yes and No, or a more complex Likert Scale that consists of three or more choices. You can create Polling tool in Visual Basic easily by using the option buttons. In our program, the users are given five choices, Excellent, Very Good, Good, Satisfactory and Bad. The results are presented in frequency and percentage respectively.

In this example, you can include a graphical display of the percentages of the five scores using the Line method. The syntax to draw the rectangular bars in a picture box is

```
Picture1.Line (x1, y1)-(x2, y2), color, BF
```

Where (x1, y1) is the coordinates of the upper left corner of the bar and

(X2, y2) is the coordinates of the lower right corner of the bar.

To show the bar length according to the percentage, you can use a certain value to multiply the decimal value of each score and put it under x2.

Finally, you can use the Picture1.Cls method to clear the picture box in order to refresh the drawing.

The Code

```
Dim total, Excel_total, VG_total, G_total, Sat_total, Bad_total As Integer
Dim Excel_percent, VG_percent, G_percent, Sat_percent, Bad_percent As Single
Dim done As Boolean
```

```vb
Private Sub cmd_Vote_Click()
Picture1.Cls
If Option_Excel.Value = True Then
Excel_total = Excel_total + 1
Lbl_ExcelTotal = Excel_total
ElseIf Option_VG.Value = True Then
VG_total = VG_total + 1
Lbl_VGTotal = VG_total
ElseIf Option_G.Value = True Then
G_total = G_total + 1
Lbl_GTotal = G_total
ElseIf Option_Sat.Value = True Then
Sat_total = Sat_total + 1
Lbl_SatTotal = Sat_total
ElseIf Option_Bad.Value = True Then
Bad_total = Bad_total + 1
Lbl_BadTotal = Bad_total
End If
total = Excel_total + VG_total + G_total + Sat_total + Bad_total
Lbl_Total = total
Excel_percent = Excel_total / total
VG_percent = VG_total / total
G_percent = G_total / total
Sat_percent = Sat_total / total
Bad_percent = Bad_total / total
Lbl_Excel.Caption = Format(Excel_percent, "Percent")
Lbl_VG.Caption = Format(VG_percent, "Percent")
Lbl_G.Caption = Format(G_percent, "Percent")
Lbl_Sat.Caption = Format(Sat_percent, "Percent")
Lbl_Bad.Caption = Format(Bad_percent, "Percent")
Picture1.Line (100, 750)-(3800 * Excel_percent, 950), vbRed, BF
Picture1.Line (100, 1450)-(3800 * VG_percent, 1650), vbMagenta, BF
Picture1.Line (100, 2150)-(3800 * G_percent, 2350), vbGreen, BF
Picture1.Line (100, 2850)-(3800 * Sat_percent, 3050), vbBlue, BF
Picture1.Line (100, 3550)-(3800 * Bad_percent, 3750), vbYellow, BF
End Sub
```

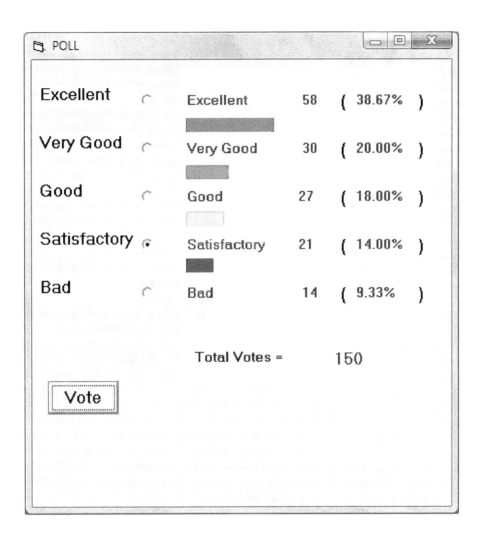

6.5 Digital Stopwatch

You can design a stopwatch so that it resembles a typical digital stopwatch. When the user clicks mode, he or she can select clock, date and stopwatch. When he or she selects clocks, the current time is displayed and when date is selected, the current date will be displayed. Lastly, when the user selects the stopwatch, all the digits will be set to 0 so that it can be used as a stopwatch.

In this program, you need to insert one label, three command buttons and two timers. The interval of timer1 which is used for the stopwatch and you need to set the interval at 1(1000th of a second). Timer2 will be used to display the clock and the interval will be set at 1000(or 1 second). Besides, you can also use six string variables to display the digits of the stopwatch so that you can put in the colons ":" and the decimal point. Now, you need to create a subroutine known as countime

The code

```
Dim a As String
Dim b As String
Dim c As String
Dim x As String
Dim y As String
Dim z As String
Dim h As String
Dim m As String
Dim s As String
Dim u As String
Dim v As String

Public interval As Double
Private Sub clock_Click()
Timer1.Enabled = False
Timer2.Enabled = True
End Sub
```

```
Private Sub Command1_Click()
Timer1.Enabled = True
Timer1.interval = 1
End Sub


Private Sub Command2_Click()
Timer1.Enabled = False
End Sub


Private Sub Command3_Click()
Timer1.Enabled = False
a = "0"
b = "0"
c = "0"
x = "0"
y = "0"
z = "0"
u = "0"
v = "0"


h = a + b
m = c + x
s = y + z
'To set the display as "00:00:00.00"
Label1.Caption = h + ":" + m + ":" + s + "." + u + v
End Sub


Sub counttime()
If Val(v) < 9 Then
v = v + 1
Label1.Caption = a + b + ":" + c + x + ":" + y + z + "." + u + v
ElseIf Val(u) < 9 Then
v = 0
u = u + 1
Label1.Caption = a + b + ":" + c + x + ":" + y + z + "." + u + v
ElseIf Val(z) < 9 Then
v = 0
u = 0
z = z + 1
Label1.Caption = a + b + ":" + c + x + ":" + y + z + "." + u + v
```

```
ElseIf Val(y) < 5 Then
v = 0
u = 0
z = 0
y = y + 1
Label1.Caption = a + b + ":" + c + x + ":" + y + z + "." + u + v
ElseIf Val(x) < 9 Then
v = 0
u = 0
z = 0
y = 0
x = x + 1
Label1.Caption = a + b + ":" + c + x + ":" + y + z + "." + u + v
ElseIf Val(c) < 5 Then
v = 0
u = 0
z = 0
y = 0
x = 0
c = c + 1
Label1.Caption = a + b + ":" + c + x + ":" + y + z + "." + u + v
ElseIf Val(b) < 9 Then
v = 0
u = 0
z = 0
y = 0
x = 0
c = 0
b = b + 1
Label1.Caption = a + b + ":" + c + x + ":" + y + z + "." + u + v
ElseIf Val(b) < 9 Then
v = 0
u = 0
z = 0
y = 0
x = 0
c = 0
b = b + 1
Label1.Caption = a + b + ":" + c + x + ":" + y + z + "." + u + v
ElseIf Val(a) < 9 Then
v = 0
```

```
u = 0
z = 0
y = 0
x = 0
c = 0
b = 0
a = a + 1
Label1.Caption = a + b + ":" + c + x + ":" + y + z + "." + u + v
End If
End Sub


Private Sub date_Click()
Label1.Caption = Date
Timer2.Enabled = False
End Sub


Private Sub Form_Load()

a = "0"
b = "0"
c = "0"
x = "0"
y = "0"
z = "0"
u = 0
v = 0
h = a + b
m = c + x
s = y + z
'To set the display as "00:00:00.00"
Label1.Caption = h + ":" + m + ":" + s + "." + u + v
End Sub


Private Sub stopwc_Click()
Timer2.Enabled = False
a = "0"
b = "0"
c = "0"
x = "0"
y = "0"
z = "0"
```

```
u = "0"
v = "0"

h = a + b
m = c + x
s = y + z
Label1.Caption = h + ":" + m + ":" + s + "." + u + v
End Sub


Private Sub Timer1_Timer()
counttime
End Sub


Private Sub Timer2_Timer()
Label1.Caption = Time
End Sub
```

To add the menu items to the interface, you need to add them from the menu editor, as shown below:

The Interface

6.6 Choice Selection Program

Very often when you visit a website, you are presented with a list of choices for you to select. Choice selection can easily be programmed in Visual Basic; the control that you can use is the check box. The status of the checkbox is either checked or unchecked, and the syntax is Checkbox1.Value=VbChecked or Checkbox1.Value=vbUnchecked. In the following program, you can construct a three-choice selection list. After the user made the selection, a message box will appear to display the list of selected choices

The Code

```vb
Private Sub Command1_Click()
If Check1.Value = vbChecked And Check2.Value = vbChecked And
Check3.Value = vbChecked Then
MsgBox ("You like Reading, Computer and Sports")
ElseIf Check1.Value = vbChecked And Check2.Value = vbChecked And
Check3.Value = vbUnchecked Then
MsgBox ("You like Reading and Computer")
ElseIf Check1.Value = vbChecked And Check2.Value = vbUnchecked And
Check3.Value = vbChecked Then
MsgBox ("You like Reading and Sports")
ElseIf Check1.Value = vbUnchecked And Check2.Value = vbChecked And
Check3.Value = vbChecked Then
MsgBox ("You like Computer and Sports")
ElseIf Check1.Value = vbChecked And Check2.Value = vbUnchecked And
Check3.Value = vbChecked Then
MsgBox ("You like Reading and Sports")
ElseIf Check1.Value = vbChecked And Check2.Value = vbUnchecked And
Check3.Value = vbUnchecked Then
MsgBox ("You like Reading only ")
ElseIf Check1.Value = vbUnchecked And Check2.Value = vbChecked And
Check3.Value = vbUnchecked Then
MsgBox ("You like computer only")
ElseIf Check1.Value = vbUnchecked And Check2.Value = vbUnchecked
And Check3.Value = vbChecked Then
```

```
MsgBox ("You like Sports only")
Else
MsgBox ("You have no hobby")
End If
End Sub
```

The Interface

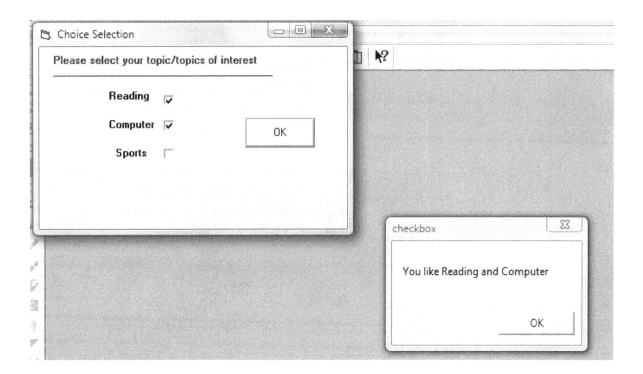

7 Database Applications

7.1 Simple Database Management System

This is a simple database management system that stores data using a text file. First of all, the program will check whether the text file is open or not and if the file does not exist, the program prompts the user to create the file by displaying the create button.

However, if the file is already there, the program will change the caption of the create button to open file. The program uses Append in the place of Output so that new data will be added to the end of the file instead of overwriting the old data. The program will also show the input box repeatedly so that the user can enter data continuously until he or she enters the word "finish".

The program also introduces the error handler to handle errors while reading the file or deleting the file because the program cannot read or delete the file when the file has not been created. The syntax for error handler is **On Error Goto** Label where the label is an error handling sub procedure. For example, when the program is trying to read the file when the file does not exist, it will go the label file_error and the error handling object **'err'** will display an error message with its description property which takes the format **err.description**. The program uses the **vbCrLf** constant when reading the data so that the data will appear line by line instead of a continuous line. The vbCrLf constant is equivalent to the pressing of the Enter key (or return key) so that the next data will go to the newline. The program is uses the Do…Loop to read all the data until it reaches the end of the file by issuing the command Loop While Not EOF.

The Code

```
Dim studentname As String
Dim intMsg As String


Private Sub Command1_Click()
'To read the file
Text1.Text = ""
Dim variable1 As String
On Error GoTo file_error
Open "C:\My Folder\sample.txt" For Input As #1
Do
Input #1, variable1
Text1.Text = Text1.Text & variable1 & vbCrLf
Loop While Not EOF(1)
Close #1


Exit Sub
file_error:
MsgBox (Err.Description)
End Sub


Private Sub Command2_Click()

'To delete the file
On Error GoTo delete_error
Kill "D:\Liew Folder\sample.txt"
Exit Sub
delete_error:
MsgBox (Err.Description)
End Sub

Private Sub create_Click()
'To create the file or open the file for new data entry
Open "D:\MyFolder\sample.txt" For Append As #1
intMsg = MsgBox("File sample.txt opened")
```

```
Do
studentname = InputBox("Enter the student Name or type finish to
end")
If studentname = "finish" Then
Exit Do
End If
Write #1, studentname & vbCrLf
intMsg = MsgBox("Writing " & studentname & " to sample.txt ")
Loop
Close #1
intMsg = MsgBox("File sample.txt closed")


End Sub


Private Sub Form_Load()
On Error GoTo Openfile_error
Open "D:\ MyFolder\sample.txt" For Input As #1
Close #1
Exit Sub
Openfile_error:
MsgBox (Err.Description), , "Please create a new file"
create.Caption = "Create File"
End Sub
```

The Interface

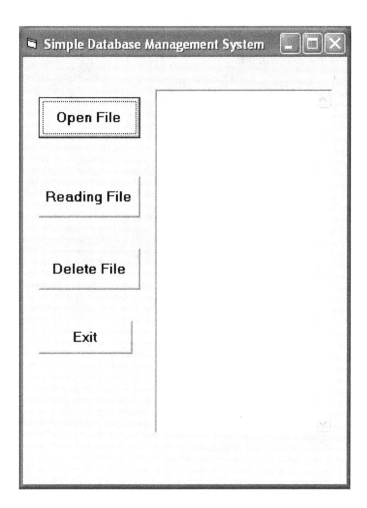

7.2 A Simple Database Application

In this example, you will create a simple database application which enables the user to browse customers' names. To create this application, insert the data control into the new form. Place the data control somewhere at the bottom of the form. Name the data control as data_navigator.To be able to use the data control, you need to connect it to any database. You can create a database file using any database application but I suggest you use the database files that come with VB6. Let's select **NWIND.MDB** as the database file.

To connect the data control to this database, double-click the **DatabaseName** property in the properties window and select the above file. Next, double-click on the **RecordSource** property to select the customers' table from the database. You can also change the caption of the data control to anything but I use "Click to browse Customers" here. After that, insert a label and change its caption to Customer Name.

Finally, insert another label and name it as cus_name and leave the label empty as customers' names will appear here when the user clicks the arrows on the data control. You need to bind this label to the data control for the application to work. To do this, open the label's **DataSource** and select data_navigator, which will appear automatically. One more thing that you need to do is to bind the label to the correct field so that data in the field will appear on the label. To do this, open the **DataField** property and select ContactName. Now, press F5 and run the program. You should be able to browse all the customers' names by clicking the arrows on the data control.

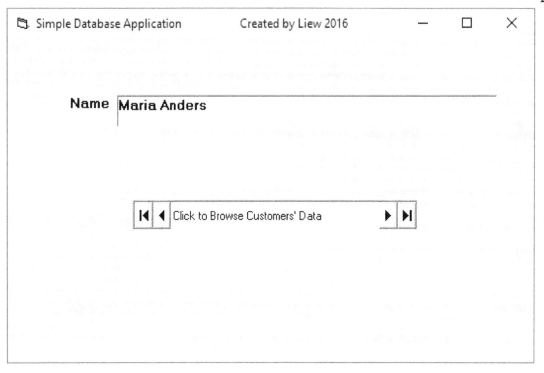

Now you shall modify the same application to make it a little more advanced database management system. The data control supports some methods that are useful in manipulating the database, for example, moving the pointer to a certain location. The following are some of the commands that you can use to move the pointer around.

data_navigator.RecordSet.MoveFirst   ' Move to the first record

data_navigator.RecordSet.MoveLast   ' Move to the last record

data_navigator.RecordSet.MoveNext   ' Move to the next record

data_navigator.RecordSet.Previous   ' Move to the first record

*note: data_navigator is the name of the data control

Now, insert four command buttons and label them as First Record, Next Record, Previous Record and Last Record. They will be used to navigate the database without using the data control. You still need to retain the same data control (from example in lesson 19) but set the property Visible to False so that users will not see the data control but use the buttons instead to browse through the database .Double-click on the command button and enter the code below:

```
Private Sub CmdMoveFirst_Click ()
dtaBooks.Recordset.MoveFirst
End Sub

Private Sub CmdMoveNext_Click ()
     dtaBooks.Recordset.MoveNext
End Sub

Private Sub CmdMovePrev_Click ()
dtaBooks.Recordset.MovePrevious
End Sub

Private Sub CmdMoveLast_Click ()
dtaBooks.Recordset.MoveLast
End Sub
```

Run the application and you will obtain the interface below and you will be able to browse the database using the four command buttons.

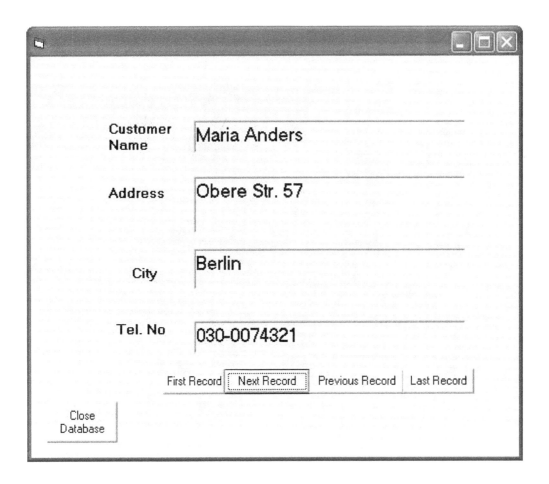

7.3 A Library Management System

You have learned how to build VISUAL BASIC database applications using data control. However, data control is not a very flexible tool as it works only with limited kinds of data and must work strictly in the Visual Basic environment. To overcome these limitations, you can use a much more powerful data control in VISUAL BASIC known as ADO control. ADO stands for ActiveX data object. As ADO is ActiveX-based, it can operate on different platforms. Besides, it can access many different kinds of data such as web-based data displayed in Internet browsers, email text and even graphics other than the usual relational and non-relational database information. To be able to use ADO data control, you need to insert it into the toolbox. To do this, simply press Ctrl+T to open the components dialog box and select Microsoft ActiveX Data Control 6. From here you can proceed to build the ADO-based **Library Management System.**

First of all, name the new form as FormLibrary and change its caption to Library Management System. Secondly, insert the ADO data control and name it as adoBooks and change its caption to book. Next, insert the necessary labels, text boxes and command buttons. The runtime interface of this program is shown in the figure below; it allows adding and deleting as well as updating and browsing of data.

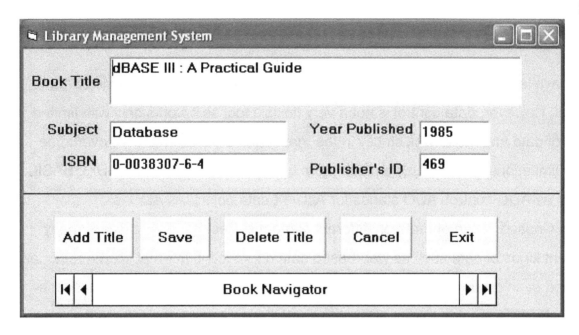

The properties of all the controls are listed in the following table:

Object	Property
Form	Name : FormLibrary Caption: Book Titles -Library Management System
ADO	Name :AdoLibrary
Label1	Name : Titlelbl Caption: Book Title
Label2	Name: Subjectlbl Caption : Subject :Year Published:
Label3	Name: Yearlbl Caption : Year Published
Label 4	Name : ISBNlbl Caption :ISBN
Labe5	Name : PubIDlbl

	Caption :Publisher's ID:
Text1	Name : Titletxt DataField :Title DataSource :AdoLibrary
Text3	Name: YearTxt DataField :Year Published DataSource: AdoLibrary
Text3	Name : ISBNTxt DataField :ISBN DataSource : AdoLibrary
Text4	Name: Pubtxt DataField : PubID DataSource: AdoLibrary
Text2	Name : Subject Txt DataField : Subject DataSource: AdoLibrary
Command Button1	Name :save Caption :Save
Command Button2	Name : add Caption: Add
Command Button3	Name: delete Caption: Delete
Command Button4	Name : cancel Caption :&Cancel
Command Button5	Name: exit

	Caption :Exit

To be able to access and manage a database, you need to connect the ADO data control to a database file. You will use the access database file **BIBLIO.MDB** that comes with VB6. To connect ADO to this database file, follow the steps below:

a) Click on the ADO control on the form and open up the properties window.

b) Click on the **ConnectionString** property and the following dialog box will appear.

When the dialog box appears, select Use Connection String. Next, click build and at the Data Link dialog box, double-click the option labeled **Microsoft Jet 3.51 OLE DB provider**.

After that, click the Next button to select the file **BIBLO.MDB**. You can click on Test Connection to ensure proper connection of the database file. Click OK to finish the connection. Finally, click on the **RecordSource** property and set the command type to **adCmd** Table and Table name to **Titles**.

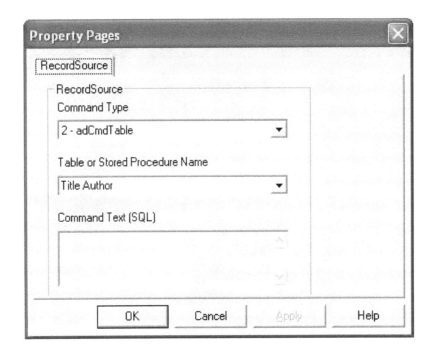

Now, you need to write codes for all the command buttons, after which you can make the ADO control invisible.

For the Save button, the procedure code is as follows:

```
Private Sub save_Click()
On Error GoTo errSave
AdoLibrary.Recordset.Fields("Title") = TitleTxt.Text
AdoLibrary.Recordset.Fields("Year Published") = YearTxt.Text
AdoLibrary.Recordset.Fields("ISBN") = ISBNTxt.Text
AdoLibrary.Recordset.Fields("PubID") = PubTxt.Text
AdoLibrary.Recordset.Fields("Subject") = SubjectTxt.Text
AdoLibrary.Recordset.Update
Exit Sub
errSave:
MsgBox (Err.Description)
End Sub
```

For the Add button, the procedure code is as follows:

```
Private Sub Add_Click()
On Error GoTo addErr
AdoLibrary.Recordset.AddNew
Exit Sub
addErr:
MsgBox (Err.Description)
End Sub
```

For the Delete button, the procedure code is as follows:

```
Private Sub delete_Click()
Confirm = MsgBox("Are you sure you want to delete this record?",
vbYesNo, "Deletion Confirmation")
If Confirm = vbYes Then
On Error GoTo deleteErr
AdoLibrary.Recordset.delete
MsgBox "Record Deleted!",, "Message"
Else
MsgBox "Record Not Deleted!", , "Message"
End If
Exit Sub
deleteErr:
MsgBox (Err.Description), , "Empty record, please enter all the
info"
End Sub
```

For the Cancel button, the procedure is as follows:

```
Private Sub cancel_Click()
TitleTxt.Text = ""
YearTxt.Text = ""
PubTxt.Text = ""
ISBNTxt.Text = ""
SubjectTxt.Text = ""
End Sub
```

Now you shall enhance the library management system by adding some new features such as a welcome dialog, a registration dialog, a login dialog and SQL search capabilities. The registration dialog will accept users' registrations and the login dialog will handle a login command that requires the user to enter a password, thus enhancing the security aspect of the database management system. Basically, the application will constitute a welcome menu, a registration menu, a login menu and the main database menu. The sequence of the dialogs is illustrated in the flowchart below:

First, insert a form and design it as the Welcome menu as shown in the figure below. In this form, insert three command buttons and set their properties as listed in the table below.

Object	Name	Caption
Form name	main_menu	Electronic Library
command button 1	cmdRegister	Register
command button 2	cmdLogin	Login

command button 3	cmdCancel	Cancel

The procedure code for the welcome menu is shown below:

```vb
Private Sub cmdLogin_Click ()
main_menu.Hide
Login_form.Show
End Sub
Private Sub cmdRegister_Click ()
main_menu.Hide
Register. Show
End Sub
```

If a new user clicks the Register button, the registration form will appear. This registration form consists of two text boxes, three command buttons and an ADO control. Their properties are listed in the table and the interface is shown in the figure below. Note that the PasswordChar of the Text2 textbox is set as * to hide the real passwords from others.

Object	Property
Form	Name :Register Caption: Registration Form
Text1	Name: txtName
Text2	Name: txtpassword
Text2	PasswordChar : *
command button 1	Name :cmdConfirm Caption: Confirm
command button 2	Name: cmdClear

	Caption: Clear
command button 3	Name: cmdCancel
	Caption: Cancel
ADO control name	Name :UserInfo

Registration Form

Enter Your name :

Enter Your Password :

Confirm   Clear   Cancel

In order to connect the ADO to a database, you must create a database file in Microsoft Access. The database file must contain at least two fields, one for the user name and the other one for the password. The procedure code for the registration form is as follows:

```
Private Sub cmdClear_Click ( )
txtName.Text = ""
txtpassword.Text = ""
End Sub
Private Sub cmdConfirm_Click ()
UserInfo.Recordset.Fields ("username") = txtName.Text
UserInfo.Recordset.Fields ("password") = txtpassword.Text
UserInfo.Recordset.Update
Register. Hide
Login_form.Show
```

```
End Sub
Private Sub Form_Load ()
UserInfo.Recordset.AddNew
End Sub
```

The login dialog is illustrated in the figure below:

There are two text boxes and a command button on the Login form. Their properties are set as follows:

Object	Property
Text1	Name: txtName
Text2	Name: txtpassword PasswordChar *
Command button 1	Name: cmdLogin Caption: Login
Form name	Name: Login form

	Caption: Login Menu	

The procedure code is as follows:

```
Private Sub cmdLogin_Click()
Dim usrname As String
Dim psword As String
Dim usernam As String
Dim pssword As String
Dim Msg As String
Register.UserInfo.Refresh
usrname = txtName.Text
psword = txtpassword.Text

Do Until Register.UserInfo.Recordset.EOF
If Register.UserInfo.Recordset.Fields ("username").Value = usrname
And Register.UserInfo.Recordset.Fields ("password").Value = psword
Then
Login_form.Hide
frmLibrary.Show
Exit Sub
Else
Register.UserInfo.Recordset.MoveNext
End If
Loop
Msg = MsgBox ("Invalid password, try again!", vbOKCancel)
If (Msg = 1) Then
Login_form.Show
txtName.Text = ""
txtpassword = ""
Else
Unload Me
End If
End Sub
```

Now you shall modify the library management system interface and add even more features to it. You shall add the following components:

- Database navigation buttons
- Microsoft DataGrid Control 6.0
- Search Box

The properties of the command buttons are set as shown in the table on next page.

Object	Property
Command button 1	Name: cmdFirst Caption: First Record
Command button 2	Name: cmdNext Caption: Next Record
Command button 3	Name: cmdPrevious Caption: Previous Record
Command button 4	Name: cmdLast Caption: Last Record
Command button 5	Name: cmdViewAll Caption: View All Records
Label1	Name: LblSearch Caption: Search
Option Button1	Name: Opt_ISBN Caption: ISBN
Option Button 2	Name: Opt_Author

	Caption: Author
Option Button 3	Name: Opt_Title
	Caption: Title
Microsoft DataGrid Control 6.0	Name: DataLibrary

The code for the navigation buttons is as follows:

```
Private Sub cmdFirst_Click()
AdoLibrary.Recordset.MoveFirst
End Sub
Private Sub cmdLast_Click()
AdoLibrary.Recordset.MoveLast
End Sub
Private Sub cmdNew_Click()
AdoLibrary.Recordset.AddNew
End Sub


Private Sub cmdNext_Click()
AdoLibrary.Recordset.MoveNext
End Sub


Private Sub cmdPrevious_Click()
AdoLibrary.Recordset.MovePrevious
End Sub
```

To add search and query capability to the library management system, you can use SQL (Structured Query Language). To be able to use SQL with Visual Basic, you have to connect the Visual Basic application to the database library.mdb using the following statements under the Form_Load procedure:

```
'To connect to MS Access database library.mdb
AdoLibrary.ConnectionString = "
Provider=Microsoft.Jet.OLEDB.4.0;Data Source=C:\My Documents\VB
```

```
Program\library.mdb;Persist Security Info=False"
AdoLibrary.RecordSource = "SELECT * FROM book"
AdoLibrary.Refresh
Set DataLibrary.DataSource = AdoLibrary
AdoLibrary.Refresh
```

*You have to change the path of your database file to the actual path of the database file in your computer.

The code for SQL queries based on ISBN, author and book title is as follows:

```
Dim SearchString As String
SearchString = TxtSearch.Text

'Search for ISBN that is same as SearchString
If Opt_ISBN.Value = True Then
AdoLibrary.RecordSource = "SELECT * FROM book WHERE ISBN='" &
SearchString & "'"

ElseIf Opt_Author.Value = True Then
'Search for author name that starts with first alphabet of
SearchString
AdoLibrary.RecordSource = "SELECT * FROM book WHERE Author Like '"
& SearchString & "%'"

ElseIf Opt_Title.Value = True Then
'Search for Title that starts with first alphabet of SearchString
AdoLibrary.RecordSource = "SELECT * FROM book WHERE Title Like '"
& SearchString & "%'"
```

Explanations:

SELECT * means select ALL the records, FROM means to select information from a certain table, WHERE is the keyword that set the conditions of the query while LIKE and % are used together to search for information that begins the with first alphabet of SearchSrting

The complete code for the SQL search and the DataGrid is as follows:

```
Private Sub cmdSearch_Click()
Dim SearchString As String
SearchString = TxtSearch.Text

If Opt_ISBN.Value = True Then
AdoLibrary.RecordSource = "SELECT * FROM book WHERE ISBN='" &
SearchString & "'"
ElseIf Opt_Author.Value = True Then
AdoLibrary.RecordSource = "SELECT * FROM book WHERE Author Like '"
& SearchString & "%'"
ElseIf Opt_Title.Value = True Then
AdoLibrary.RecordSource = "SELECT * FROM book WHERE Title Like '"
& SearchString & "%'"
End If

AdoLibrary.Refresh
'To reset the column width of datagrid DataLibrary
With DataLibrary
.Columns(0).Width = 2200
.Columns(1).Width = 4500
.Columns(2).Width = 2800
.Columns(3).Width = 2000
.Columns(4).Width = 800
.Columns(5).Width = 1500
End With

End Sub


Private Sub CmdViewAll_Click()
AdoLibrary.RecordSource = "SELECT * FROM book"
AdoLibrary.Refresh
```

```
'To reset the column width of datagrid DataLibrary
With DataLibrary
.Columns(0).Width = 2200
.Columns(1).Width = 4500
.Columns(2).Width = 2800
.Columns(3).Width = 2000
.Columns(4).Width = 800
.Columns(5).Width = 1500
End With


End Sub


Private Sub Form_Load()
'To connect to MS Access database library.mdb
AdoLibrary.ConnectionString = "
Provider=Microsoft.Jet.OLEDB.4.0;Data Source=C:\ My Documents\ VB
Program\library.mdb;Persist Security Info=False"
AdoLibrary.RecordSource = "SELECT * FROM book"
AdoLibrary.Refresh
Set DataLibrary.DataSource = AdoLibrary
AdoLibrary.Refresh


'To Set the alignment of the window to center of screen
Left = (Screen.Width - Width) \ 2
Top = (Screen.Height - Height) \ 2


'To set the alignment of the datagrid to centre of form
DataLibrary.Left = (Form1.Width - DataLibrary.Width) \ 2


'To set the column width of datagrid DataLibrary
With DataLibrary
.Columns(0).Width = 2200
.Columns(1).Width = 4500
.Columns(2).Width = 2800
.Columns(3).Width = 2000
.Columns(4).Width = 800
.Columns(5).Width = 1500
End With


End Sub
```

The Interface

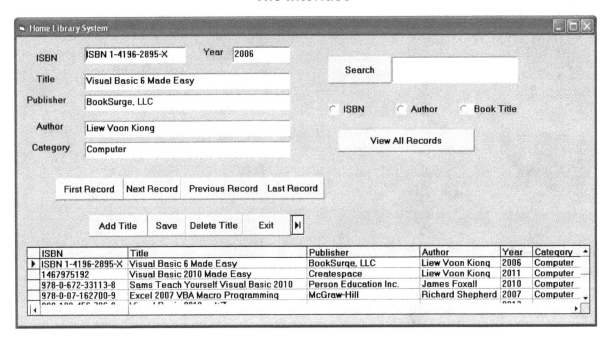

7.4 Inventory Management System

All businesses involve inventory and need to manage it efficiently to ensure smooth running of the business activities and profitability. To manage inventory efficiently, business owners need to develop a good inventory management system. Building a sound inventory management system usually incurs high cost. Fortunately, you can use Visual Basic 6 to build an inventory management system which does not require big capital; you can do it at home. In Visual Basic 6, there are a number of built-in database management tools which you can use to manage the data.

To start building a good inventory system, you need to have good planning. First of all, you have to sit down with your client to get detail information about his or her businesses and establish the kind of system he or she wants. For example, you need to know what types of goods they are dealing with, the turn-over volumes, cost prices, selling prices and more. Besides that, you need to know what kind of documents the system needs to deal with like invoices, delivery orders and more.

After getting all the necessary information from your client, you can then start to build a database. Based on the number and types of products, you need to decide what are the variables or fields needed to be included in the database's tables. You shall use a hypothetical case to illustrate how to build an inventory system as shown above. Let's say our client is dealing with electrical goods.

Step 1: Creating the database tables

To design the database tables, you need to determine how many tables are needed. In order to keep things simple, you shall limit to two tables in our example.
The first table shall be used to store the data of the inventory or stock in hand. The second table shall be used to record stocks coming in and stocks going out.

The first table shall comprise the following fields:

- Category
- Brand
- Item Description
- Model Number
- Stock
- Unit Cost

The second table shall comprise the following fields:

- Date
- Category
- Brand
- Item Description
- Model Number
- Stock In
- Stock Out
- Unit Cost
- Total Cost

In our example, you can name the first table **Inventory** and the second table **Stock** .After designing the tables, you can then proceed to create a database that comprises the two tables. You can either use Microsoft Access to create the database or you can use the built-in **Visual Data Manager** in Visual Basic 6. Visual Data Manager can be used to create tables, add new data as well as edit data. Besides that, it can be used to modify table structure. To learn how to create database using Visual Data Manager, follow the link below:

http://www.vbtutor.net/index.php/creating-database-using-visual-data-manager/

Step 2: Inserting controls into Form

The next step is to insert some relevant controls into the form for displaying and manipulating the data of the database. The controls to be inserted are **ADO data controls**, **DataGrid controls**, **FlexGrid control** and various command buttons. DataGrid control and FlexGrid control are used to display and store the data from the database tables. On the other hand, ADO data control is used to manipulate the database such as connecting the DataGrid and FleGrid to the database.

To be able to use ADO data control, you need to insert it into the toolbox. To do this, simply press Ctrl+T to open the components dialog box and select **Microsoft ActiveX Data Control 6**. After this, you can proceed to build your ADO-based VB database applications. In our example, you need to insert two ADO data controls and name them **AdoInventory** and **AdoStock** respectively. The first is to deal with data in the Inventory table and the second is to deal with data in the Stock table. Besides, you can also insert two DataGrid controls and named them **DataInventory** and **DataStock** respectively. They are used to display the data to the user. Finally, you can insert one FlexiGrid control to store the data and also to print out the data by connecting it to MS Excel spreadsheet.

Step 3: Writing the Code

After inserting the necessary controls, it is time to write code to coordinate the controls and to manipulate the data. The first most important code for our program is to connect the ADO data controls to the database when the form is loaded. It comprises SQL syntax like SELECT and FROM. The code is as follows:

```
Private Sub Form_Load()
'To connect AdoInventory to MS Access database inventory_br.mdb
AdoInventory.ConnectionString = "
```

```
Provider=Microsoft.Jet.OLEDB.4.0;Data Source=C:\My
Documents\inventory_br.mdb;Persist Security Info=False"
AdoInventory.RecordSource = "SELECT * FROM Inventory"
AdoInventory.Refresh
Set DataInventory.DataSource = AdoInventory
'To connect AdoStock to MS Access database inventory_br.mdb
AdoStock.ConnectionString = "
Provider=Microsoft.Jet.OLEDB.4.0;Data Source=C:\ My
Documents\inventory_br.mdb;Persist Security Info=False"
AdoStock.RecordSource = "SELECT * FROM Stock"
AdoStock.Refresh
Set DataStock.DataSource = AdoStock
```

Notice that you can use SQL syntax **SELECT * FROM** to select all the data from the Inventory table and the stock table. SQL is a powerful language that is used to manipulate databases.

The next code is to let user enter data into the **DataInventory** table and double click to update the data as well as to calculate the total cost. It also adds brands and categories into the **brand combo box** and the **category combo box** respectively .The code is as follows:

```
Private Sub DataInventory_DblClick()
Dim TotalCost As Integer
If AdoInventory.Recordset.Fields("CPU") <> "" Then
TotalCost = Val(AdoInventory.Recordset.Fields("CPU")) *
Val(AdoInventory.Recordset.Fields("Stock"))
AdoInventory.Recordset.Fields("TCost") = Str(TotalCost)
Else
AdoInventory.Recordset.Fields("TCost") = ""
End If
```

```
'To load all brands into comboBrand
'To load all Categories into comboCategory
Do Until AdoInventory.Recordset.EOF
ReDim B(i), C(j) As String
B(i) = AdoInventory.Recordset.Fields("Brand")
C(j) = AdoInventory.Recordset.Fields("Category")
ComboBrand.AddItem B(i)
ComboCategory.AddItem C(j)
AdoInventory.Recordset.MoveNext
Loop
AdoInventory.Recordset.MoveFirst
End Sub
```

You can also write the code to search for the items once they are entered into the inventory table. The code is as follows:

```
'Search for items using SQL query

Dim SearchString1, SearchString2 As String
SearchString1 = ComboBrand.Text
SearchString2 = ComboCategory.Text
If ComboBrand.Text <> "All Brands" And ComboCategory.Text <> "All
Categories" Then
AdoInventory.RecordSource = "SELECT * FROM Inventory WHERE
Brand='" & SearchString1 & "' and Category='" & SearchString2 &
"'"
ElseIf ComboBrand.Text = "All Brands" And ComboCategory.Text <>
"All Categories" Then
AdoInventory.RecordSource = "SELECT * FROM Inventory WHERE
Category='" & SearchString2 & "'"
ElseIf ComboBrand.Text <> "All Brands" And ComboCategory.Text =
"All Categories" Then
AdoInventory.RecordSource = "SELECT * FROM Inventory WHERE
Brand='" & SearchString1 & "'"

ElseIf ComboBrand.Text = "All Brands" And ComboCategory.Text =
```

```
"All Categories" Then
AdoInventory.RecordSource = "SELECT * FROM Inventory"
End If
AdoInventory.Refresh
```

Next, you need to write code for entering new item in **DataStock** table. The code is as follows:

```
'To add items to Ado Stock
AdoStock.Recordset.AddNew
AdoStock.Recordset.Fields("Date") = Format(Date, "dd/mm/yyyy")
AdoStock.Recordset.Fields("Category") =
AdoInventory.Recordset.Fields("Category")
AdoStock.Recordset.Fields("Brand") =
AdoInventory.Recordset.Fields("Brand")
AdoStock.Recordset.Fields("Item Description") =
AdoInventory.Recordset.Fields("Item Description")
AdoStock.Recordset.Fields("Model Number") =
AdoInventory.Recordset.Fields("Model Number")
AdoStock.Recordset.Fields("CPU") =
AdoInventory.Recordset.Fields("CPU")
AdoStock.Recordset.Update
```

Please note that AddNew is to allow adding new data and Update is to save data.

The Code

```
'To set border styles for Excel
Private Enum ExlBorderAround
xlHairline = 1
xlMedium = -4138
xlThick = 4
xlThin = 2
xlColorIndexAutomatic = -4105
End Enum
Private Sub CmdEnd_Click()
End
 Sub


Private Sub CmdConvert_Click()
Dim hex_val As String
Dim trueVal As Double

hex_val = AdoStock.Recordset.Fields("TCost")
'To convert hexadecimal to decimal value
trueVal = CInt("&H" & hex_val)
Text1.Text = Str(trueVal)
End Sub
```

```
Private Sub CmdCpu_Click()
Dim CostPU As String
CostPU = InputBox("Enter Unit Cost")
AdoStock.Recordset.Fields("CPU") = Str(Val(CostPU))
AdoStock.Recordset.Fields("TCost") =
Str(Val(AdoStock.Recordset.Fields("Out")) * Val(CostPU))
AdoInventory.Recordset.Update
AdoStock.Recordset.Update
End Sub


Private Sub CmdDo_Click()
'To sum up all the values in column 9 of the Flexigrid
Dim mysum As Double
Dim nrow As Integer
Dim r As Integer
nrow = MSFlexGrid1.Rows 'To count all the rows in MSFlexiGrid1
For r = 0 To nrow - 1
mysum = mysum + Val(MSFlexGrid1.TextMatrix(r, 9))
Next


Text1.Text = Str(mysum)
'To add last line to Flexigrid table that shows total cost
MSFlexGrid1.AddItem "" & vbTab & "" & vbTab & "" & vbTab & "" &
vbTab & "" _
& vbTab & "" & vbTab & "" & vbTab & "" & vbTab & "Total Cost" &
vbTab & Str(mysum)


'Printing Delivery order Via Excel
Dim ObjExcel As Object
Dim wbk As Object
Dim wst As Object
Dim i%
Dim myrow, mycol, noofusedrows As Integer
Set ObjExcel = CreateObject("Excel.Application")
Set wbk = ObjExcel.Workbooks.Add
Set wst = wbk.ActiveSheet


'This Adds a new workbook, you could open the workbook from file
also


Clipboard.Clear 'Clear the Clipboard With MSFlexGrid1
```

```
'Select Full Contents (You could also select partial content)
.Col = 0 'From first column
.Row = 0 'From first Row (header)
.ColSel = .Cols - 1 'Select all columns
.RowSel = .Rows - 1 'Select all rows
Clipboard.SetText .Clip 'Send to Clipboard
End With


With ObjExcel.Application.ActiveSheet
.Range("A1").EntireColumn.Columnwidth = 8 'Set Columnwidth for
column1=10
.Range("B1").EntireColumn.Columnwidth = 10
.Range("C1").EntireColumn.Columnwidth = 8
.Range("D1").EntireColumn.Columnwidth = 10
.Range("E1").EntireColumn.Columnwidth = 12
.Range("F1").EntireColumn.Columnwidth = 4
.Range("G1").EntireColumn.Columnwidth = 4
.Range("H1").EntireColumn.Columnwidth = 6
.Range("I1").EntireColumn.Columnwidth = 10
.Range("J1").EntireColumn.Columnwidth = 6
.Range("F1").EntireColumn.HorizontalAlignment = 2
.Range("G1").EntireColumn.HorizontalAlignment = 2
'Select Cell A1 (will paste from here, to 'different cells)
'Paste clipboard contents
.Range("A1").Select .Paste noofusedrows = wst.UsedRange.Rows.Count
'To get number of used 'rows
'To set borders for the selected cells
For myrow = 2 To noofusedrows
For mycol = 1 To 10
wst.Cells(myrow, mycol).BorderAround , ExlBorderAround.xlThin,
ExlBorderAround.xlColorIndexAutomatic, vbBlack
Next
Next
'To set borders for the last row
wst.Range(.Cells(noofusedrows + 1, 1), .Cells(noofusedrows + 1,
10)).BorderAround , ExlBorderAround.xlThin,
ExlBorderAround.xlColorIndexAutomatic, vbBlack
.PrintOut 'To print out the selection
End With
End Sub
```

```vb
Private Sub CmdExit_Click()
    Unload Me
End Sub
Private Sub CmdIn_Click()
Dim hex_val As String
Dim StockValue
AdoStock.Recordset.Fields("In") = InputBox("Enter Stock In")
StockValue = Val(AdoStock.Recordset.Fields("In")) +
Val(AdoInventory.Recordset.Fields("Stock"))
AdoInventory.Recordset.Fields("Stock") = Str(StockValue)
AdoInventory.Recordset.Update
AdoStock.Recordset.Update
End Sub


Private Sub cmdNew_Click()
'Add new item to stock
Dim MsgInstr As Integer
MsgInstr = MsgBox("Have you selected one item from Stock List? If
YES, Click OK to Proceed", vbYesNoCancel + vbQuestion, "Select
Item")
If MsgInstr = 6 Then
Timer4.Enabled = True
Else
Timer4.Enabled = False
End If
End Sub


Private Sub Cmdout_Click()
'Enter total item out
Dim StockValue
AdoStock.Recordset.Fields("Out") = InputBox("Enter Stock Out")
StockValue = Val(AdoInventory.Recordset.Fields("Stock")) -
Val(AdoStock.Recordset.Fields("Out"))
AdoInventory.Recordset.Fields("Stock") = Str(StockValue)

AdoInventory.Recordset.Update
AdoStock.Recordset.Update
End Sub
```

```vb
Private Sub CmdSearch_Click()
'Search for items using SQL query
Dim SearchString1, SearchString2 As String
SearchString1 = ComboBrand.Text
SearchString2 = ComboCategory.Text


If ComboBrand.Text <> "All Brands" And ComboCategory.Text <> "All
Categories" Then
AdoInventory.RecordSource = "SELECT * FROM Inventory WHERE
Brand='" & SearchString1 & "' and Category='" & SearchString2 &
"'"
ElseIf ComboBrand.Text = "All Brands" And ComboCategory.Text <>
"All Categories"  Then
AdoInventory.RecordSource = "SELECT * FROM Inventory WHERE
Category='" & SearchString2 & "'"
ElseIf ComboBrand.Text <> "All Brands" And ComboCategory.Text =
"All Categories"  Then
AdoInventory.RecordSource = "SELECT * FROM Inventory WHERE
Brand='" & SearchString1 & "'"
ElseIf ComboBrand.Text = "All Brands" And ComboCategory.Text =
"All Categories"  Then
AdoInventory.RecordSource = "SELECT * FROM Inventory"
End If
AdoInventory.Refresh
'Formatting DataInventory (DataGrid)
With DataInventory
.Columns(0).Width = 2000 'Setting width for first column
.Columns(1).Width = 1500
.Columns(2).Width = 2500
.Columns(3).Width = 2000
.Columns(4).Width = 1200
.Columns(5).Width = 1100
.Columns(5).Caption = "Unit Cost" 'Set caption of column 8
.Columns(6).Width = 1200
.Columns(6).Caption = "Total Cost"
End With

End Sub
```

```vb
Private Sub CmdView_Click()
'View all items
AdoInventory.RecordSource = "SELECT * FROM Inventory"
AdoInventory.Refresh
End Sub


Private Sub Command2_Click()
AdoInventory.Recordset.Update
End Sub


Private Sub Command3_Click()
AdoInventory.Recordset.Delete
End Sub


Private Sub Command4_Click()
If AdoStock.Recordset.BOF = False Then
AdoStock.Recordset.Delete

Else
MsgBox ("No Item to Delete")
End If
End Sub


Private Sub Command5_Click()
AdoInventory.Refresh.Refresh
End Sub


Private Sub ComboBrand_DropDown()
Timer1.Enabled = False
End Sub


Private Sub ComboCategory_DropDown()
Dim i, j As Integer
Do Until i = ComboCategory.ListCount
For j = 1 To ComboCategory.ListCount - i - 1
If ComboCategory.List(j + i) = ComboCategory.List(i) Then

ComboCategory.RemoveItem j + i

End If
Next
```

```vb
i = i + 1
Loop
End Sub



Private Sub Command1_Click()
Dim r, nrow As Integer
Dim mysum As Double
nrow = MSFlexiGrid1.Rows
For r = 0 To nrow - 1
mysum = mysum + Val(MSFlexiGrid1.TextMatrix(nrow, 9))
Next
End Sub


Private Sub DataInventory_AfterUpdate()
Dim TotalCost As Integer
If AdoInventory.Recordset.Fields("CPU") <> "" Then
TotalCost = Val(AdoInventory.Recordset.Fields("CPU")) *
Val(AdoInventory.Recordset.Fields("Stock"))
AdoInventory.Recordset.Fields("TCost") = Str(TotalCost)
Else
AdoInventory.Recordset.Fields("TCost") = ""
End If
End Sub


Private Sub DataInventory_DblClick()
If AdoInventory.Recordset.Fields("CPU") <> "" Then
Dim TotalCost As Integer
TotalCost = Val(AdoInventory.Recordset.Fields("CPU")) *
Val(AdoInventory.Recordset.Fields("Stock"))
AdoInventory.Recordset.Fields("TCost") = Str(TotalCost)
Else
AdoInventory.Recordset.Fields("TCost") = ""
End If
'To load all brands into comboBrand
'To load all Categories into comboCategory
Do Until AdoInventory.Recordset.EOF
ReDim B(i), C(j) As String
B(i) = AdoInventory.Recordset.Fields("Brand")
C(j) = AdoInventory.Recordset.Fields("Category")
```

```
ComboBrand.AddItem B(i)
ComboCategory.AddItem C(j)
AdoInventory.Recordset.MoveNext
Loop
AdoInventory.Recordset.MoveFirst
End Sub


Private Sub DataStock_Click()
Dim TotalCost As Integer
If AdoStock.Recordset.Fields("Out") <> "" Then
TotalCost = Val(AdoStock.Recordset.Fields("CPU")) *
Val(AdoStock.Recordset.Fields("Out"))
AdoStock.Recordset.Fields("TCost") = Str(TotalCost)
End If
End Sub


Private Sub DataStock_DblClick()
'To populate the MSFlexiGrid with data from Adostock in different
columns
'whenever the user clicks the row in dataStock
MSFlexGrid1.Visible = True
Dim DateStr, CategoryStr, BrandStr, MoNumStr, ItemStr, OutStr,
InString, BranchStr, CostStr, TCostStr, AllCostStr, linetext As
String
Dim AllCost As Double
DateStr = AdoStock.Recordset.Fields("Date") 'To assign the value
in Date field 'to DateStr
CategoryStr = AdoStock.Recordset.Fields("Category")
BrandStr = AdoStock.Recordset.Fields("Brand")
MoNumStr = AdoStock.Recordset.Fields("Model Number")
ItemStr = AdoStock.Recordset.Fields("Item Description")
OutStr = AdoStock.Recordset.Fields("Out")
InStrng = AdoStock.Recordset.Fields("In")
BranchStr = AdoStock.Recordset.Fields("Branch")
CostStr = AdoStock.Recordset.Fields("CPU")
TCostStr = AdoStock.Recordset.Fields("TCost")
AllCost = AllCost + Val(TCostStr)
AllCostStr = Str(AllCost)

linetext = DateStr & vbTab & CategoryStr & vbTab & BrandStr &
```

```
vbTab & _
MoNumStr & vbTab & ItemStr & vbTab & InStrng & vbTab & OutStr &
vbTab & BranchStr & vbTab & _
CostStr & vbTab & TCostStr & vbTab & AllCostStr


MSFlexGrid1.ColWidth(0) = 1200 'sets the first column width to
1000.
MSFlexGrid1.ColWidth(1) = 1500 'sets the Second column width to
2500.
MSFlexGrid1.ColWidth(2) = 1500 'sets the Third column width to
1500.
MSFlexGrid1.ColWidth(3) = 1600 'sets the Fourth column width to
1600.
MSFlexGrid1.ColWidth(4) = 2000 'sets the Fifth column width to
3000.
MSFlexGrid1.ColWidth(5) = 500 'sets the Sixth column width to
2000.
MSFlexGrid1.ColWidth(6) = 500 'sets the Seven column width to 500.
MSFlexGrid1.ColWidth(7) = 600 'sets the Seven column width to
1000.
MSFlexGrid1.ColWidth(8) = 800 'sets the Seven column width to
1000.
MSFlexGrid1.ColWidth(9) = 600 'sets the Seven column width to
1000.


'To set columns alignments
Dim ColAlign As Integer
For ColAlign = 0 To 9
MSFlexGrid1.ColAlignment(ColAlign) = flexAlignLeftTop
Next
MSFlexGrid1.AddItem linetext
AdoStock.Recordset.Update
End Sub


Private Sub Form_Load()


'To connect to MS Access database inventory_br.mdb
AdoInventory.ConnectionString = "
Provider=Microsoft.Jet.OLEDB.4.0;Data Source=C:\My
Documents\inventory_br.mdb;Persist Security Info=False"
AdoInventory.RecordSource = "SELECT * FROM Inventory"
```

```
AdoInventory.Refresh
Set DataInventory.DataSource = AdoInventory


'To connect to MS Access database inventory_br.mdb
AdoStock.ConnectionString = "
Provider=Microsoft.Jet.OLEDB.4.0;Data Source=C:\Documents and
Settings\Voon Kiong Liew\My Documents\Liew Folder\Bunga
Raya\inventory_br.mdb;Persist Security Info=False"
AdoStock.RecordSource = "SELECT * FROM Stock"
AdoStock.Refresh
Set DataStock.DataSource = AdoStock



'To set the alignment of the windows to centre of screen
Left = (Screen.Width - Width) \ 2
Top = (Screen.Height - Height) \ 2


'To set the alignment of the datagrid to centre of Form
DataInventory.Left = (Form1.Width - DataInventory.Width) \ 2
DataStock.Left = (Form1.Width - DataStock.Width) \ 2
'To load all brands into comboBrand
ComboBrand.Text = "All Brands"
ComboBrand.AddItem "All Brands"


'To load all Categories into comboCategory
ComboCategory.Text = "All Categories"
ComboCategory.AddItem "All Categories"


Do Until AdoInventory.Recordset.EOF
ReDim B(i), C(j) As String
B(i) = AdoInventory.Recordset.Fields("Brand")
C(j) = AdoInventory.Recordset.Fields("Category")


ComboBrand.AddItem B(i)
ComboCategory.AddItem C(j)
AdoInventory.Recordset.MoveNext


Loop


AdoInventory.Recordset.MoveFirst
'Formatting DataInventory (DataGrid)
```

```
With DataInventory
.Columns(0).Width = 2000 'Setting width for first column
.Columns(1).Width = 1500
.Columns(2).Width = 2500
.Columns(3).Width = 2000
.Columns(4).Width = 1200
.Columns(5).Width = 1100
.Columns(5).Caption = "Unit Cost" 'Set caption of column 8
.Columns(6).Width = 1200
.Columns(6).Caption = "Total Cost"
End With


'Formatting DataStock (DataGrid)
With DataStock
.Columns(0).Width = 1500 'Setting width for first column
.Columns(1).Width = 2000
.Columns(2).Width = 1500
.Columns(3).Width = 2500
.Columns(4).Width = 1800
.Columns(5).Width = 600
.Columns(6).Width = 600
.Columns(7).Width = 1100
.Columns(8).Width = 1100
.Columns(8).Caption = "Unit Cost" 'Set caption of column 8
.Columns(9).Width = 1200
.Columns(9).Caption = "Total Cost"
End With


End Sub


'Add item brand to combo box


Private Sub Timer1_Timer()
Dim i, j As Integer
Do Until i = ComboBrand.ListCount
For j = 1 To ComboBrand.ListCount - i - 1
If ComboBrand.List(j + i) = ComboBrand.List(i) Then
ComboBrand.RemoveItem j + i
End If
Next
i = i + 1
```

```vb
Loop
End Sub


Private Sub Timer2_Timer()
'Add category to combo box
Dim i, j As Integer
Do Until i = ComboCategory.ListCount
For j = 1 To ComboCategory.ListCount - i - 1
If ComboCategory.List(j + i) = ComboCategory.List(i) Then
ComboCategory.RemoveItem j + i ' To remove duplicated items
End If
Next
i = i + 1
Loop
End Sub


Private Sub Timer3_Timer()
Timer1.Enabled = False
Timer2.Enabled = False
Timer3.Enabled = False
End Sub


Private Sub Timer4_Timer()
'To add items to Ado Stock
AdoStock.Recordset.AddNew
AdoStock.Recordset.Fields("Date") = Format(Date, "dd/mm/yyyy")
AdoStock.Recordset.Fields("Category") =
AdoInventory.Recordset.Fields("Category")
AdoStock.Recordset.Fields("Brand") =
AdoInventory.Recordset.Fields("Brand")
AdoStock.Recordset.Fields("Item Description") =
AdoInventory.Recordset.Fields("Item Description")
AdoStock.Recordset.Fields("Model Number") =
AdoInventory.Recordset.Fields("Model Number")
AdoStock.Recordset.Fields("CPU") =
AdoInventory.Recordset.Fields("CPU")
AdoStock.Recordset.Update
Timer4.Enabled = False
End Sub
```

8. Internet Applications

8.1 Web Browser

If you are bored with your existing web browsers, you might want to create your very own web browser using Visual Basic. To create the web browser, you have to press Ctrl+T to open up the components window and select **Microsoft Internet Control**. After you have selected the control, you will see the control appear in the toolbox as a small globe. To insert the Microsoft Internet Control into the form, just drag the globe into the form and a white rectangle will appear in the form. You can resize this control as you wish. This control is given the default name **WebBrowser1**.

To design the interface, you need to insert one combo box which will be used to display the URLs. In addition, you need to insert a few images which will function as command buttons for the user to navigate the Internet; they are the **Go** command button, the **Back** command button, the **Forward** command button, the **Refresh** command button and the **Home** command button. You can actually put in the command buttons instead of the images, but using images will definitely improve the look of the browser.

The procedures for all the commands are relatively easy to write. There are many methods, events, and properties associated with the web browser but you need to know just a few of them to come up with a functional Internet browser. They are listed in the following table:

Method	Description
GoBack	To navigate backward one page in the history list.
GoForward	To navigate forward one page in the history list.

GoHome	To navigate to the default start page.
GoSearch	To navigate to the current search page.
Navigate	To navigate to the URL or to the file identified by a full path.
Refresh	To reload the file that is currently loaded.
Stop	To cancel the current web page loading operation.
Properties	
Busy	To indicate whether the web browser is engaged in navigation or downloading operations.
LocationName	To retrieve the name of the document that Internet Explorer is currently displaying.
LocationURL	To retrieve the URL of the web page that Internet Explorer is currently displaying.
Event	
DocumentComplete	Executed when a document has been completely loaded.
DownloadBegin	Executed when a navigation operation begins.
DownloadComplete	Executed when a navigation operation finishes.
FileDownload	Executed to indicate that a file download is about to occur.
NavigateComplete	Executed after navigation to a link is completed.

The method navigate is to go the website specified by its Uniform Resource Locator (URL). The syntax is **WebBrowser1.Navigate ("URL").** In this program, if you want to load **www.vbtutor.net** web page at start-up, you can enter this address in the URL slot. The code is

```
Private Sub Form_Load()
WebBrowser1.Navigate ("http://www.vbtutor.net")
End Sub
```

To show the URL in the combo box and also to display the page title at the form caption after the page is completely loaded, we can use the following statements:

```
Private Sub WebBrowser1_DocumentComplete (ByVal pDisp As Object,
URL As Variant)
Combo1.Text = URL
Form1.Caption = WebBrowser1.LocationName
Combo1.AddItem URL
End Sub
'The following procedure will tell the user to wait while the page
is loading.

Private Sub WebBrowser1_DownloadBegin ()
Combo1.Text = "Page loading, please wait"
End Sub
```

The Code

```
Private Sub Form_Load ()
WebBrowser1.Navigate ("http://www.vbtutor.net")
End Sub

Private Sub Image1_Click ()
WebBrowser1.GoHome
End Sub

Private Sub Image2_Click ()
On Error Resume Next
WebBrowser1.GoForward
End Sub

Private Sub Image3_Click ()
```

```vb
On Error Resume Next
WebBrowser1.GoBack
End Sub

Private Sub Image4_Click ()
WebBrowser1.Refresh
End Sub

Private Sub Image5_Click ()
WebBrowser1.Stop
End Sub

Private Sub Label2_Click ()
WebBrowser1.Navigate (Combo1.Text)
End Sub

Private Sub Label4_Click ()
WebBrowser1.GoSearch
End Sub

Private Sub WebBrowser1_DocumentComplete(ByVal pDisp As Object,
URL As Variant)
Combo1.Text = URL
Form1.Caption = WebBrowser1.LocationName
Combo1.AddItem URL
End Sub

Private Sub WebBrowser1_DownloadBegin()
Combo1.Text = "Page loading, please wait"
End Sub
```

The Interface

8.2 FTP Program

File Transfer Protocol (FTP) is a system for transferring files between two computers over the Internet where one of the computers is known as the server and the other one as the client. FTP program is very useful for website management as it allows the webmaster to update web pages by uploading local files to the web server easily . For normal PC users, FTP program can also be used to download files from many FTP sites that offer a lot of useful stuffs such as free software, free games, product information, applications, tools, utilities, drivers, fixes and etc.

FTP program usually comprises an interface that shows the directories of the local computer and the remote server. Files can be transferred just by clicking the relevant arrows. To log into the FTP site, you have to enter the username and the password; however, for public domains, you just need to type the word anonymous as the username and you can leave out the password. The FTP host name takes the form ftp.servername.com, for example, the Microsoft FTP site's host name is ftp.microsoft.com . FTP program usually provides a set of commands such as **ChgDir** (changing directory), **MkDir** (Changing directory), **Rename** (renaming a file), **view** (to view a file), **delete** (to delete a file) etc.

If you need to use a FTP program, you can purchase one or you can download a couple of the programs that are available free of charge over the Internet. However, you can also create your very own FTP program with Visual Basic. Visual Basic allows you to build a fully functionally FTP program which may be just as good as the commercial FTP programs. The engine behind it is **Microsoft Internet Transfer Control 6.0** in which you need to insert into the form before you can create the FTP program. The name of the Microsoft Internet Transfer Control 6.0.is **Inet** and if you only put in one control, its name is **Inet1.**

Inet1 comprises three important properties namely **Inet1.URL** which is used to identify the FTP hostname, **Inet1.UserName** which is used to accept the username and the **Inet1.Password** which is used to accept the user's passwords. The statements for the program to read the hostname of the server, the username and the password entered into the TxtURL textbox, the TxtUserName textbox and the TxtPassword textbox by the user are shown below:

```
Inet1.URL=Text1.Text
Inet1.UserName=Text2.Text
Inet1.Passoword=Text3.Text
```

After the user enters the above information, the program will attempt to connect to the server using the following command, where **Execute** is the method and DIR is the FTP command that will read the list of files from the specified directory of the remote computer and you need to use the **getChunk** method to actually retrieve the directory's information.

```
Inet1.Execute, "DIR"
```

After connecting to the server, you can choose the file to download from the remote computer by using the statement

```
Inet1.Execute, , "get" & remotefile & localfile
```

Where **remotefile** is the file of the remote site and **localfile** is the file of the local system. However, very often you need to provide the full path of the local file, which you can do that by modifying the above syntax to the following syntax:

```
Inet1.Execute , , "get" & remotefile & localpath & remotefile
```

The above statements will ensure that the remote file will be downloaded to the location specified by the localpath and the file downloaded will assume the same name as the remote file. For example, the remote file is **readme.txt** and the localpath is **C:\temp** , so the downloaded file will be saved in **C:\temp\readme.txt.**

In order to monitor the status of the connection, you can use the **StateChanged** event that is associated with Inet1 together with a set of the state constants that are listed in the following table:

Constant	Value	Description
icHostResolvingHost	1	The control is looking up the IP address of the specified host computer.
icHostResolved	2	The control successfully found the IP address of the specified host computer.
icConnecting	3	The control is connecting to the host computer.
icConnected	4	The control successfully connected to the host computer.
icRequesting	5	The control is sending a request to the host computer.
icRequestSent	6	The control successfully sent the request.
icReceivingResponse	7	The control is receiving a response from the host computer.
icResponseReceived	8	The control successfully received a response from the host computer.
icDisconnecting	9	The control is disconnecting from the host computer.
icDisconnected	10	The control successfully disconnected from the host computer.

icError	11	An error occurred in communicating with the host computer.
icResponseCompleted	12	The request has been completed and all data has been received.

Under the **StateChanged** event, you can use the Select Case...End Select statements to notify the users regarding the various states of the connection. The procedure is as follows:

```
Private Sub Inet1_StateChanged(ByVal State As Integer)
Select Case State
Case icError
MsgBox Inet1.ResponseInfo, , "File failed to transfer"
Case icResolvingHost
Label6.Caption = "Resolving Host"
Case icHostResolved
Label6.Caption = "Host Resolved"
Case icConnecting
Label6.Caption = "Connecting Host"
Case icConnected
Label6.Caption = "Host connected"
Case icReceivingResponse
Label6.Caption = "Receiving Response"
Case icResponseReceived
Label6.Caption = "Got Response"
Case icResponseCompleted
Dim data1 As String
Dim data2 As String
MsgBox "Download Completed"
End Select
End Sub
```

The states of the connection will be displayed on Label6.

The FTP program also contains a form and a dialog box. The dialog box can be added by clicking on the Project item on the menu bar and then selecting the Add Form item on the drop-down list. You can either choose a normal dialog box or a login dialog box. The function of the dialog box is to accept the FTP address, the username and the password and then to establish connection to the server. After a successful login, the dialog box will be hidden and the main form will be presented to the user to browse the remote directory and to choose certain files to download. The interface of the login dialog is shown in following figure:

The states of the connection will be displayed on the label at the bottom. The program for the login dialog is:

```
Option Explicit

Private Sub OKButton_Click()
Inet1.URL = Text1.Text
Inet1.UserName = Text2.Text
Inet1.Password = Text3.Text
Inet1.Execute , "DIR"
Form1.Show
```

```
Dialog.Hide
End Sub


Private Sub Inet1_StateChanged(ByVal State As Integer)
Select Case State
Case icError
MsgBox Inet1.ResponseInfo, , "File failed to transfer"
Case icResolvingHost
Label6.Caption = "Resolving Host"
Case icHostResolved
Label6.Caption = "Host Resolved"
Case icConnecting
Label6.Caption = "Connecting Host"
Case icConnected
Label6.Caption = "Host connected"
Case icReceivingResponse
Label6.Caption = "Receiving Response"
Case icResponseReceived
Label6.Caption = "Got Response"
Case icResponseCompleted
Dim data As String
Dim data1 As String

MsgBox "Transfer Completed"
Do
   data1 = Inet1.GetChunk(1024, icString)
   data = data & data1

Loop While Len(data1) <> 0
    Form1.Text6.Text = data
End Select
End Sub
Private Sub CancelButton_Click()
Text1.Text = ""
Text2.Text = ""
Text3.Text = ""
End Sub
```

The statement **data1 = Inet1.GetChunk (1024, icString)** is to use the getChunk method to grab information of the remote directory and then display the files of the directory in the Text6 textbox.

After successful log in, the main form will be presented as shown in the following figure:

The program code to download the file is:

```
Dim remotefile As String
Dim mypath As String
Dim cmd As String
Private Sub Command1_Click ()
remotefile = Text4.Text
```

```
mypath = Text5.Text
cmd = "GET " & remotefile & " " & mypath & remotefile
Inet1.Execute , cmd
End Sub
Private Sub Command2_Click ()
Inet1.Cancel
End
End Sub


Private Sub Form_Load ()
Dialog.Show
Form1.Hide
End Sub


Private Sub Inet1_StateChanged (ByVal State As Integer)
Select Case State
Case icError
MsgBox Inet1.ResponseInfo, , "File failed to transfer"
Case icResponseCompleted
MsgBox "Download Completed"
End Select
End Sub
```

INDEX

www.ingramcontent.com/pod-product-compliance
Lightning Source LLC
Chambersburg PA
CBHW080634060326
40690CB00021B/4929